Sekhmet Rising

The Restlessness of Women's Genius

"what a ride"
p. 84.

Sekhmet Rising

The Restlessness of Women's Genius

Louise LeBrun

With 17 Amazing Women!

 WEL-Systems Institute

© 2006 Louise LeBrun, WEL-Systems Institute

First Edition, June 2006

Published by:

WEL-Systems® Institute
260 Hearst Way, Suite 210
Ottawa, Ontario, Canada   K2L 3H1

Voice: 613 254-7218
Toll Free (Canada and USA): 1-877-233-2005
Website: www.WEL-Systems.com
E-mail: info@WEL-Systems.com

All rights reserved.

No part of this book may be reproduced or transmitted in any form or by any means without prior written consent of the The WEL-Systems Institute, excepting brief quotes used in connection with reviews written specifically for inclusion in magazines, newspaper or the internet.

Louise LeBrun, WEL-Systems Institute, owns the copyright for the *Sekhmet Rising book project.* Each contributor retains the personal copyright of her own individual contribution.

WEL-Systems®, Quantum TLC™, The CODE Model™, CODE Model Coach™ are registered trademark or trademarks of Louise LeBrun, WEL-Systems Institute and are used with permission.

Library and Archives Canada Cataloguing in Publication

LeBrun, Louise, 1950-

  Sekhmet rising: the restlessness of women's genius / Louise LeBrun with 17 amazing women.

  ISBN 0-9688064-4-9

     1. Women--Psychology. 2. Self-actualization (Psychology). I. Title

  BF637.S4L3679 2006   158.1'082   C2006-902895-8

Printed in Canada

Dedication

*To the women
who are showing us the way
to redefine our humanity
and reshape our destiny.*

Also by Louise LeBrun

FULLY ALIVE:
Creating A Life that Invites Health,
Humour, Compassion and Truth

PHOENIX RISING:
The Freeing of Human Potenial

WHEN THE HORSE DIES, GET OFF...
and Stop Dragging It Around!

Table of Contents

PREFACE
    Louise LeBrun 1

SEKHMET RISES: THE GODDESS AWAKENS
    Louise LeBrun 9

COMING TO THE EDGE
    Karina Evangelista 17

A WAKE-UP CALL
    Dorothy Spence 29

BURSTING INTO FLAME
    Eva Marsh 45

MOMENTS IN AN INDIAN GIRL'S LIFE
    Harjit Shokar 59

DANCING AROUND THE FIRE
    Susan Griffin 73

THE PASSAGE BACK TO ME
    Koreen Kimakowich 87

WALKING THE LABYRINTH
    Anita Allen 105

CONNECTING WITH THE GENIUS
    Theresa McKeown 119

EMBRACING THE FIRE WITHIN
    Carole MacInnis 131

BETWEEN CATERPILLAR AND BUTTERFLY
    Dominique Dennery 147

VOLCANOES AND FOOLS
    Gwen McCauley 161

UNLEASHED !
    Noreen Mejias 175

THE JOURNEY HOME
    Jackie Zirpdji 195

FINDING MY MAGIC... WITHIN
    Patricia Donihee 211

ONE WOMAN'S LIFE CHOICE
    Céline Burlock 227

THE PROMISE OF COMING HOME
    Susan Bremner 243

IT'S NEVER TOO LATE TO REDESIGN YOUR LIFE
    Lorna LeBrun 255

REFLECTIONS
    All Contributors 271

Preface

Louise LeBrun

I have spent much of my life in the company of women. They have been my family and friends; my bosses and employees; my competitors and mentors; my students and my teachers but most of all, each has been a playmate in the game of our choosing. They have been my greatest challenges, my staunchest supporters and my most formidable opponents. This book is a celebration of each and every one of these women and testimony to the innate genius of who they are.

Sekhmet Rising: The Restlessness of Women's Genius creates the space for women who have awakened to and claimed their own potential to share their experience with you. But these women are going further than their own awakening and are choosing to be seen, heard and experienced by you in their commitment to awaken others. Awaken you to your own potential. Awaken you to that which lies deep inside your being and aches to be seen and heard and expressed. It may well be that for each of us, there comes a time when that force is so compelling we become unwilling and unable to be silent – and the sound of who we are spills over into all that we do, all that we have become and makes its way through the world.

The energy that is Sekhmet lives inside each of us. The force of that presence cannot be silenced indefinitely without the inevitable death – first of spirit, then of mind and finally of body – that is its natural consequence. Its unrelenting surges through the body will either awaken us or silence us forever as it tears through tissue and thought, either transforming or destroying all in its path. The women in this book have chosen to live!

Through more than 25 years of working with women, I have learned to trust the restlessness of women's genius. In those moments when all around us would have affixed labels of 'victim', 'loser' or 'crazy', without exception, as we chose to stay with what was moving… inside, where we lived… the restless nature of their 'issues' would ultimately become the beacon that would guide them home. Home to themselves and to the discovery of what was meaningful for them, in their lives. In the moment of that discovery, their 'issues' would disappear.

Each of the women who are contributing to this book has engaged in at least one WEL-Systems® based experience. Each has had to come face-to-face with herself; not just who she wanted to be but who she had already become. In that moment of awakening, each stood in the stillpoint, watching… noticing… and creating the space not only to choose from existing options but creating new ones and in so doing, inviting potential by choice and by intention. In the instant of their courage came the opportunity and the invitation to become MORE!

Each of these women is unique, sharing her experience with you in the hope that you will discover more of yourself. In her own words and through the 'sound' of her own voice, each of these women begins by sharing with you what life was like for her before she discovered and claimed that deep, inner knowing and brought it to life in the choices she made. As she stepped into that undeniable truth of who she is and in so doing, became more authentically herself, her life began to change as did the lives of all she touched.

Their stories are not only of their random evolution but are also of evolution by intention and its impact on the world they shape. Their journeys have not been easy ones. They were required to let go… to trust the truth of their own experience… to find within themselves the internal point of reference that would allow them to live larger and more powerful lives. They had to let go... to leave some people behind... and be willing to journey alone. And through it all, what they discovered was that although their journey was theirs and theirs alone, they were never by themselves. As they stood tall and looked around, they found each other. In that collective of choice came companionship and strength.

This book is offered as the Sacred Space within which these women tell their stories. They have become willing to be seen and heard – and unwilling any longer to hide and be silent about the truth of who they are and the truth of their own experience.

These women are awake! And beyond that, they have the desire to awaken those other women whose sleep is disturbed by that restlessness from deep within; disturbed by the force that moves through them – *the energy that is Sekhmet* – rising from somewhere deep in the belly, preparing to give birth to a world of their own choosing.

These women are courageous. They are strong and powerful. Like they are warm and supportive and loving, they are also fierce in their determination never again to be leashed or caged; to be silenced and invisible. Their commitment to themselves and to no longer hiding who they are is greater than any fear they carry.

Alone, each is a ripple of possibility in the world. Together, as they create, engage in and expand this living organic collective, they become a tsunami of unstoppable potential. Their discovery in the full force of their capacity to create will pave the way for them to shape new ways to co-create with each other and with those who desire a more generative, life-sustaining way to manifest their world.

Each of these women has had to find within herself the Fire that would allow her to shape her destiny and manifest a meaningful life. As they have done so, they have looked back over their lives to see - within each of the moments and each of the choices driven by fear, uncertainty and even the identity of victim - the innate genius that was present. And through it all, there was a restlessness - a wordless knowing deep within - that there was more. As they moved into this restlessness, they found themselves.

The energy that is Sekhmet is not only Crucible and Spear, it is also the Stillpoint – that place from which to bear witness and observe; from which to mindfully choose to engage rather than react or be drawn in to that which will not serve us. The Stillpoint is the space within which to stand… to be awake and aware and without fear… and to be willing to do what is required, knowing that the power to engage is there. In those moments, we are devoid of the need to do harm – to ourselves or anyone else. The need to do so comes from the deep terror of being powerless – and *that* we are no longer!

Be well warned: these women are highly contagious! The thought virus that they have become is virulent and air-born… moving through culturally conditioned beliefs, values and attitudes and throwing wide the doors and windows that have kept us hidden; and have kept us suffocating and hostage to the limitations of our own thoughts.

Each of these powerful women comes from a time in her life when she did not know who she was. Things changed… they discovered… they changed their lives… and now they share their journey with you that you might discover a place of your own power from which to create your world.

I am deeply honoured to call these women my friends. I have been privileged to journey with them as they stepped into the process of discovery of their own power. It is with a joyous heart that I engage with them to bring you the invitation and the encouragement to find the same within yourself. Know that as you do so, you are not alone.

As women, the genius we carry is not only of the intellect. As schooled, experienced and credentialed as we are, we also know that the intellect is far more limited in its potential than is intuition. Intellect will allow you to manage what is; intuition will allow you to envision and manifest what might become. When we begin to trust the truth of our own experience; when we begin to trust the power of the body, as we do during gestation and birth, we become that which sources potential beyond the limitations of logic and reason. We delight in our unreasonableness and allow the unknown to guide us through the dilemmas of our own making. We become able to determine mindfully that which is authentic to the truth of our experience and choose to direct the evolution of our lives from the intention of who we will become. And life changes – rapidly and profoundly.

In these turbulent and uncertain times, we stand at a critical point of our own evolution. Will we do as so many who have come before us have chosen to do and look back on our history to determine what future we will create? Or will we choose to stand in the NOW and look forward… declaring to ourselves and all who surround us that we choose to move into our future clearly focused, intending to manifest from our potential and not from our fears and our limitations; or from what we think we've been conditioned for or deserve. Consider for a moment the power of contagion of an awakened organic collective. What becomes possible for us all as we create and manifest meaningful lives worth living? It is not enough for us to breed and replicate. We must also discover that which will allow us to unfold by choice and intention… and encourage and welcome that discovery in others.

The energy that is Sekhmet is a call to women to awaken! It is our invitation to become mindful of every sound we make - the tone and timbre of our own voice, our choice of language, the things we say to ourselves and to each other, who we spend time in conversation with and what we say and don't say; and of every choice we engage - the things we do by choice and by obligation, the times we abandon ourselves to the opinions of others, the moments we surrender our potential to our fear; that we might mindfully notice the quality of our lives and the degree to which the outside of who we are is an accurate reflection of the inside of who we are. We must ask ourselves: Is this the truth of who I am? Does this reflect the power that I know resides inside me?

Women are the Keepers of the Flame of the future. Always have been and always will be, by virtue of the fact that we bear the next generation. Without us, there is no future. It is time for us to awaken to the potential that we carry to give birth to a new way of moving through the world.

These women open their lives to you in the hope that you will discover your own. Engage! As you read and your own thoughts awaken; as you read and the wave of recognition begins to flood your body – tears welling up from somewhere deep within – trust yourself! Your body knows exactly what to do! Let your body relax; keep your breathing long and deep and rhythmic. You focus on breathing and allowing your belly to open and soften, and the rest will unfold in its own genius. Trust the innate genius of who you are. We do.

As you read and discover, share yourself with others. Become the thought virus that breeds life and potential and a future created by choice rather than one that unfolds from habit and by default. Consider all the women in your life who would be touched by… inspired by… awakened by the lives of these women as you have been, and offer them the gift of the read. Let the lives of these women be your gift to the women and men in your life. And however you choose to do that, let your motivation be your desire to engage, reveal and bring voice to your own awakening rather than your desire to change someone else.

I believe that women MUST lead us into the future. As we allow ourselves to trust what moves inside us, we will let go of what has for far too long been considered the 'right' kind of leadership. As we relax into and claim what's already there inside us, just waiting to be freed, new forms of leadership will emerge, not because we have chosen to construct them because we ourselves have chosen to emerge from the silence within.

It is not our intellect or our knowledge that will change our lives; it is our willingness and ability to ENGAGE! As women awaken and move into their own truth, they become the invitation for men to relax into a different way of moving through their world. As women come to trust their capacity to be loving and powerful at the same time; as they relax into and reclaim their own power; as they discover that not only can they find strength and a sense of deep connection to themselves but in doing so, they deepen their connections to others, they also begin to witness that in their ability to stand alone, they gather to themselves others of shared interest and commitment – and the world changes. As we open to, embrace and trust the truth of our own experience, we become the model to our sons and daughters for the journey of their own evolution. When we betray ourselves, we are all diminished – and the world weeps.

The lives of these women matter - and so does yours.

Sekhmet Rises
The Goddess Awakens

Louise LeBrun

In a quiet moment - nestled somewhere between phone calls, emails, family feuds and general, all 'round distractions from my own inner landscape - I found myself wandering through an e-zine website. There I found articles on a variety of topics in areas of interest to women. As I browsed, something hovered just outside my awareness... not quite a distraction but more like a whispering in my mind. And then it occurred to me: the articles getting significantly more hits than the others (240 on one vs. 12 on another) were clustered around four topics:

- Digestive disorders
- Food/ fat/eating/size/weight control/management
- Depression
- Menopause

Hmm... I wondered... what's this all about? What's the message here? What is it that these 'obsessions' are trying to tell us by screaming at us through our own bodies? Each of these things has in common the sense of doing battle with or being betrayed by our own bodies.

My musings continued to lead me down a path of enquiry within my own thoughts. Are these really different and unique things or are these different expressions of the *same* thing? How else might I consider these if I were to see them as aspects of the same thing? What do all of these have in common?

What is the tapestry within which each of these is a thread of a different color or texture and yet nonetheless, all part of the same design?

And finally, the last thing that came to mind: what if the genius that my body carries (as offensive a notion as we have been taught to consider that to be!) was presenting me with messages rather than problems? Messages or invitations to be entertained and considered rather than problems or challenges to be wrestled to the ground, beaten into submission and overcome! What if these were not afflictions but were instead impossible-to-ignore markers along the path of my own evolution, letting me know what's working and what's not? How else might I need to consider myself, my world and my resourcefulness in moving through that world?

In that moment, I was reminded of the ancient Egyptian goddess, Sekhmet. In those long-ago times, in the twisting sands and scorching heat of that most mystical of places, the presence of Sekhmet flooded the awareness of Egypt and her people. With the body of a woman and the head of a lioness, there continues to exist to this day controversy about who she was, what she stood for and the meaning of her undeniable, potent presence.

For some, Sekhmet came to be associated with notions of destruction; of power gone awry, drunk with its own potential, for its own sake. And yet there persists amongst the writings that describe the force of her presence, references to her as the most ancient of the deities in the Egyptian pantheon. Regarded as the Source goddess - that which seeded all other gods and goddesses - Sekhmet represents the simultaneous presence of good and evil; of creation and destruction; of the ability and willingness to nurture and protect life, and the ability and willingness to take it away.

Hers was a presence that came to be associated with the Stillpoint - that silent, open moment of motionless engaging… watchful, awake, alive and without fear… just prior to the choosing and the will to take action as required. Her power allowed for and evoked both the Crucible and the Spear, flowing as expressions along the continuum of a single force – undivided and without conflict. Authentic… whole… aligned… and complete in her ability to choose with power and intent.

The woman's body that was Sekhmet carried the potential for creation; for birth and new life. The head of the lioness that was Sekhmet carried the portent of destruction; of danger and death reflected in the steady and piercing gaze of the hunter that she is. All that is soft, loving and nurturing and all that is dark and dangerous, rolled into one being. She is all that and much more - and so are we.

Through time, women with power - and powerful women - have often been depicted as demonstrating themselves to be unable to wield that power; devoid of the mastery required to choose with intelligence and the wisdom to exercise that power with mindfulness and force. Many are the stories that depict powerful women as evil, dangerous and harmful to creation. So completely have we mindlessly succumbed to this notion that around the world, women have become the keeper of the keys to the dungeons of our own imprisonment

Women themselves have learned to teach their sisters, daughters and each other how to be small and invisible. We have learned and now teach each other that Fire – that powerful force that moves through our bodies, screams NO and is unwilling to comply and capitulate – is dangerous to all, including ourselves and should, at all costs, be kept hidden and unexpressed or silenced completely. Worse yet, we have taught each other to hide ourselves in shame when we feel that Fire move, learning instead to lie and betray ourselves and each other rather than claim the unfamiliar territory of its expression. For some of us, we have come to question our right to feel at all.

And yet, it is well known that when lions hunt, as much as the males bellow and roar, it is the females who come together to capture and take down the kill. Their skill and precision is what allows the species to survive. It causes me to ponder:

where would we find ourselves if women were to reclaim the Fire that moves inside them; engage with each other to encourage this reclamation and move as one force to shape the world in which we live? Perhaps the time has come for us all - men and women - to reconsider what has been in order to discover what we might all become.

Over the years, in the work that I've done with women individually or in small group processes, I have often been struck by the restlessness of these women. Hidden in the conversations about relationships, children, work, parents, etc. is an underlying restlessness… an agitation… like a single, emerging thread twisting through the tapestry that is their lives. It rises to the surface to remind them that something is missing or is calling to them, then slips deeper into the fabric of their lives, lying hidden… waiting for them in those dark, long-abandoned places inside themselves, just under the veneer of their acceptable lives. This relentless restlessness keeps pressing them to pay attention to that molten, swelling Fire that flows with great force deep in the body, well below the surface of their acceptable behaviors in the world. But before they can get to it, there are two discoveries that must be moved through. These are consistent, regardless of age, economics, religious or cultural bias.

- ❖ Women are terrified of the depth of their own rage! After decades and generations of swallowing hard and holding back - years of saying 'yes' when we want to say 'no'; years of doing what someone else wants because it's just easier that way; years of not asking for what we want, surrendering what we care about, taking less than our share, being still so as not to disturb anyone else, curbing our exuberance so that we blend into the flat-lines around us; years of not trusting ourselves; of lying to keep the peace, covering our eyes so as not to see what is in front of our face… after years of swallowing back, holding in, hunkering down - it would make perfect sense that the Fire in our bodies would have gone into lock-down in some way. Better to kill ourselves slowly than to risk killing someone else, we tell ourselves.

❖ Women have bought the story - you know, the one that says 'be good, be nice, be loving and understanding, and you'll be taken care of by (fill in the blank - the husband, the culture, the system, the group, etc.) only to discover that it's all bogus! After decades of doing what we never really wanted to do anyway, we discover that we bought the goods and there's no delivery. So, not only are we enraged about that but NOW we have to learn a whole new skill set in order to be able to function effectively in the shaping of our own lives.

Fire! The Fire of our rage! The Fire of our despair! Fire moving fast and furiously! Sensations in the body that are old and familiar, yet sensations that are now moving in ways that we have no skills to manage - not because we're stupid but because no one has ever taught us how. Fire that we've been told: don't go there or you'll hurt someone's feelings… get hurt… be rejected… be left out. Don't go there because you'll be unattractive, undesirable, unwanted. And the greatest Fire of them all: don't go there because when the other women (your unspoken collective of choice and your fallback position) circle the wagon, you'll find yourself on the outside - unprotected and unsafe. Comply! Go along! Don't make waves or you make us all look bad! And we already know the brutality with which the collective will punish its own in order to maintain 'order'.

And then we wonder why our bodies start screaming at us, yanking and pulling and tearing at us - unwilling, for one more second, to be silenced by our own hand. And the restlessness grows…

Control the Fire! Control your body! Lock down! Curl in! Be silent and be still! Disconnect from yourself, if that is what it takes (depression). Silence the scream of your rage by occupying the Fire with digestion; distract yourself by directing the Fire at controlling what has come to be acceptable to be defined by others - the size and shape of your own body (food/fat/eating/size/weight). And finally, if after decades of doing so your body has become unwilling to be silenced for one more nano-second, let the Fire move - but let it fill you up and consume your reason and your measured responses to the world around you - and let it burn only you (menopause).

For what feels like eons, the exercise of power and the ability to create has often demanded of women that they choose one force at the expense of the other. And yet, there is a restlessness - inside, where we live - that will not allow us to forget the wholeness of who we are. The energy that is the Sekhmet presence in our lives - always there, always watching, always waiting for us to awaken - is the invitation for us to reclaim our natural, instinctive, innate ability to be both the Crucible and the Spear. Our natural instinctive ability to create family, community and organizational systems that honor and nurture the power of 'relationship' and its rewards (Crucible); as well as our ability to make the tough choices, draw the line in the sand, hold to our intentions and demand what we know is required to make the difference (Spear). It is not that we desire or prefer to strike; it's that we must be both able and willing to do so. Not only to protect others but for our own wellbeing, clearing the space of body, mind and soul for us to engage a meaningful life.

Get off your knees! Stand up for what we all, instinctively, know to be true of who we already are - powerful, versatile, creative innovators. Just as we are capable of great nurturing, we are also capable of taking apart that which no longer supports and sustains life. The restlessness within your own body is not disease or something wrong… it's something right! It is the invitation to rediscover and embrace the full range of your own potential; to allow yourself to reclaim the territory of those internal landscapes and to navigate by the stars of your own inner truth.

Stop apologizing for who you are! No matter your age, the color of your skin, the size of your ass or your bank account - take back who you are and what's meaningful to you in your own world! Don't wait for someone or something else to declare you free to be yourself. As long as you need permission, you are at the mercy of what you hold more powerful than yourself. As long as you need permission to be equal, you aren't.

Allow yourself to open your mouth and say what's true for you... what's real for you... and what you hold as meaningful in what sometimes feels like your meaningless existence. Only by allowing the restlessness to be fed - allowing the Fire to move! - will we ever be able to claim the life that we desire. We begin by claiming ourselves. We reach out into our families and communities and organizations, and we become the invitation for change within our collectives of choice. And with the unstoppable, combined forces of Intention and Attention, we come together to build new and larger collectives that are required to change the world.

If you're ready to play at this level of the game, there are many others just waiting to play with you. You are not alone - and the only way you'll ever know this is to step into the Fire and let it flow. The time has come for you to take your place at the table.

> A seeker for more than 25 years, Louise LeBrun creates and facilitates experiences for personal discovery and exploration. A provocative and compelling thinker, writer, speaker and educator, Louise is the Founder of the WEL-Systems Institute and author of several books and audio programs that will take you to the edge of your own awareness. Creator of the WEL-Systems® approach to change, Quantum TLC™ and The CODE Model™, she is also a Reiki Master and Huna Initiate with a passion for living and great compassion for those who desire to awaken to a more meaningful life.

Coming to the Edge

Karina Evangelista

> Come to the edge, he said
> They said, we are afraid
> Come to the edge, he said
> They came, he pushed them
> And they flew.
>
> Guillaume Apollinaire

"What an opportunity", I thought to myself, "The invitation to be willing to stand bare and fully de-cloaked." To show myself to the entire world; to reveal who I have become within this journey that I have created for myself.

The strength that I have created from within has profoundly changed my life in so many ways. I am willing to share this with the world, no matter what feelings of fear surge through the bloodstream of this new-found 'Self'. And even with all that, I wouldn't change a thing. I know that every choice along the way has been useful and has served me in some way for my own personal growth. I continue to grow, moment to moment, even as I write these words.

My very first experience was from the time of gestation being embraced by my mother's womb; being held and having my very first feeling inside myself of being safe. I remember myself as being on my back with my legs curled in, arms tight around them, as I was cradled in my mother's womb. It came time for me to come out and into the world but the intensity within my mother's body as well as my own told me I wasn't going to make it out.

At the time of my birth, I almost died. I had no choice but to put my guard up for survival. My mother was forced by doctors to not push. All I knew was that one second of my life, I was being cradled and held and the next I had my guard up for survival, not knowing as an infant what was happening. This had stayed within me, wired into my body until my present days. I have known no other way to live than with my guard up, all of my life. My guard has been up at all times, continuously fighting and protecting. Even if there was nothing to protect myself against, I would create something. This invitation, writing to all of you of my experience, is my biggest opportunity to let my guard down; to take that spear and finally put it aside so that the strength of my crucible may shine. I hold every experience within the walls of my crucible as being wide open – and that is how I want to live.

From the time I was born, from one day to the next, I remember nothing but extreme and intense experiences in my life. So intense that they were often life-threatening, teaching me over time to create a way out, to succeed and move upward in my life. I knew inside myself nothing could stop me. My memory begins at the tender age of 1 year old with being hit in the head by a swing and almost dying, to the extremely intense experience of growing up as the first daughter and child under a strict Italian roof. With the arrival of my siblings when I was 4, the intensity increased. I was expected to be the primary model for my younger sister and brother. Unknown to me then, I now realize that I had taken on the role of a family hero, taking charge and showing that I can do it. When striving to succeed and prove to my father that I could be the best model for my siblings, I would get brutally abused mentally and physically as it was never enough to please him.

In the past, I would have said that my father would find anyway possible to scare us, to the point of fear beyond belief. Today, being an adult with a very different view of the world, I can look back on these experiences and others and I look for the patterns and the metaphors to explore "Who am I really fighting, and what do I have to learn from having walked this kind of path for myself?" What intelligence could there be in these experiences, not only as a small child but even during gestation in my mother's womb? I will share with you what I experienced and by actually paying attention to my discoveries from that, who I have become today. The strength within these discoveries has been, for me, profound. So profound that I know, deep down inside, I cannot be broken; and that I can never *not* know the truth of what lies wired into my body.

For all of my life, up until maybe five years ago, I had been brought up to believe that this world is a scary place. I was brought up in extreme fear, being told every day that if I didn't abide by my father's rules, he would kill me. On a day-to-day basis, I was brought up to believe that today was another day of survival and that maybe today would be the day that I wouldn't make it.

My father would find any little possible thing to either mentally abuse us or to physically abuse us, to the extent that at the age of 5 years old, I would be dragged to the cutting board in the kitchen and my father, taking out a knife the size of a butcher's knife, would slam the knife down beside my fingers. I would be terrified every day to come home from school because I knew that he would be at home, waiting. To walk in and see that large wooden stick that he had ripped off of the bar that we used to have in our basement, that still had nails coming out of it; knowing that maybe today was the day that I'd get beaten with the wooden stick with nails at the end of it. I would pray that he would just threaten to kill me and send me to my room, even though I knew I hadn't even done anything 'bad'. I would be forced to clean the entire house everyday after school and if

I would even miss a spot, I would be sent to my room. I would be punished on a daily basis in my room with no TV, phone or music. All I had was my pencil, my paper and my cat to hold.

From the age of five, since I had nothing else around me but a pencil and paper and some crayons, I would draw. This became a huge passion within me to draw... and to draw nothing but cats, at that time. Cats and drawing were my entire life. By the age of nine, I developed my gift profoundly and I was drawing portraits. I would 'try' and use my art to get my father's attention and approval but didn't succeed. I would still feel like a failure as he would mock my work.

I continued to be threatened and still get hit but now, I would be forced to go and fetch his choice of either the stick, the belt or the shoe and bring it to him myself. Or, if he preferred, he would take me by the wrists and twist them so that I would have to bow down to him.

As the years went by, I was desperate to win his approval, either through my art or whatever other means I could think of. Nothing worked. Finally, as I aged and grew stronger within myself, there came the time when I was fed up - fed up of seeing my mother in tears, and my sister and brother, as well; fed up of hearing my mother fight with him, day after day, listening by the stairway as she fought to protect us. Every night was a struggle for her.

The time I chose to stand up for myself and stand my ground was the day I told him that if he ever laid hands on any one of us, he'd better sleep with one eye open. I was 14. The result? I spent the rest of my 14th year locked up in my bedroom most of the time. When I was 15, my parents got divorced and my sister, brother and I stayed with my mother. Interestingly enough, this is when I got really sick.

I created a disease in my body called Crohn's 'dis-ease', accompanied by severe anemia, thalassemia and a tendency to easily develop phlebitis. Crohn's is a disease that attacks both the large and small intestine. It is an extremely painful disease – and one that demands that you are always on guard for survival. Since I had nothing else to fight anymore because my father was out of the house, and I still hadn't gotten his approval or the feeling of being loved by him, Crohn's filled the void.

Both anemia and thalassemia were a lack of iron. I was always weak. Phlebitis is a blood clot that can travel in your veins. If you fall, you can create a blood clot in your leg that can travel through your artery and block your heart. All of these medical experiences were very dangerous to my health. I knew how to create HUGE things for myself. I had learned well how to live with danger over a long period of time.

Crohn's disease is considered incurable in the traditional medical model. There is no 'known' cure for Crohn's. The doctors believe that you live with it your entire life. They have no idea how it's created and they have no idea how to cure it. Well, let me tell you - I know how and I'm living proof that it is 'curable' if you really want it to be. It all depends on your perception; on whether or not you're willing to stand at cause in your life; and if you're willing to fully claim who you have been and who you can become, from this moment on.

I had Crohn's for five years, diagnosed at the age of 16 but in pain from the age of 15 – not long after I had chosen to speak up with my father and no longer silence myself. I had silenced myself throughout my entire childhood, knowing that if I spoke up the consequences would be severe. I had chosen to live differently, no matter the consequences.

Throughout these years of painful experiences and of being constantly hospitalized, I had unconsciously decided to become the 'lost child'. I dropped the role of the family hero and became the victim. I chose to close in on myself and to hide but the intensity to fight was still within me. This is the time when my mother really stood out to me in my life. Now that I'd given up the job, she became the caretaker/family hero. She did whatever she could to help me… to offer me comfort in my pain. As a Reiki Practitioner, she would offer to soothe my pain with the heat from her energy.

I became the little princess. The price however, was to live under her rules and to do as she said. But that didn't stop me - and neither did the nagging. I chose to show the world "look what you have done to me". I unconsciously used Crohn's as a way out of whatever I would create for myself. At the time, it was the best tool and most useful way for me to get what I wanted while, at the same time, telling off the world (especially my father!) for the pain I was going through; and my mother for that nagging, jabbing voice in ears.

I kept my guard up and my spear sharp, still believing that this world was a scary place. And yet, even this didn't stop me. I took on classes in illustration and design, as well as graphics, to further my career in arts. What I came to realize is that I would create experiences of authority (like my father) where I was constantly seeking approval - from my teachers, from my boyfriends and so on – from any male figure. I worked as hard as I could work to get that perfect grade. My goal was to have 'my' painting displayed so that the world could see. It came to the point where I got so sick that I had to be rushed into the hospital for an operation and take a year off of school. I was in the hospital undergoing surgery to remove a foot of my intestine as it was completely blocked and had ulcers that could have burst.

Both my parents were there, present during the operation. While I was being operated on, my grandfather on my father's side had passed away. The day after my operation, my father was there with me in the morning. I will never forget the look in his eyes that day.

A new nurse had come into my room to give me cortisone. She made a mistake and gave me the cortisone in my spine (in the epidural) rather than intravenously. I couldn't breathe and the pain was indescribable. I was clenching both sides of the bed and couldn't move or breathe because if I did, I was afraid that the staples in my stomach would rupture. The look in my father's eyes was one of fear - fear of loosing his daughter in front of his very eyes right after loosing his father that same week. All he could say was "What's wrong?!. What's wrong with you?!" as I couldn't speak.

The nurse realized what she had done and ran to get help. They had to stop the epidural completely. I was without pain killers for 10-15 minutes, just one day after I was cut open. They checked my blood pressure every 5 minutes for the next half an hour. As things settled down, I became aware of that look in my father's eyes. That look is what it took for me to actually realize that yes, my father does love me. I knew inside that I no longer needed to go out of my way to seek his approval. For me, approval had become an inside job.

My father was with me every morning; and mother, sister and brother were there every night.

One more thing: during my stay at the hospital, the one thing that I had always wanted, which was recognition of my work and for my painting to be displayed for all to see, was actually happening! My art was being displayed in the Montreal metro for everyone to see - but me. That was the hardest thing. It killed me knowing that I had achieved my goal but couldn't actually see it with my own eyes. That taught me again that success and knowing your good is an inside job. I now know that I'll not find it outside of myself.

A month after my operation, the Crohn's was back. I was deeply discouraged and ready to give up completely until one of my best friends told me "Karina, go see my aunt. Trust me." By then, I had tried everything. I had gone from 18 pills a day, to no pills, to receiving Reiki treatments from my mother and nothing would take the pain away completely. I took the chance and went to see Louise LeBrun, enrolled in a weekend program called *Phoenix Rising* that was being offered. I drove up to Ottawa in a big snow storm to spend the weekend there. All I can tell you is that $695 plus taxes to get my life back was a small price to pay!

I was in more pain then ever during the course as 'stuff' from my past and present was bumping up hard against me. I was in awe the entire time. I didn't know what to think or to feel. I found the strength and the courage to face huge things in my life that, until that moment, I had not been able to claim. By the end of the program, I was no longer willing to stand on the effect/victim side of the equation. I was no longer willing to be small.

Once I had realized how Crohn's served me and why I had created it in the first place, I knew that I no longer needed to do things 'that way'; that I actually did have a choice. I was no longer willing to use Crohn's as an easy way out or as an easy way to tell the world off for my own intelligent creation, as I knew no other way. I knew that I already had my father's attention and that the Crohn's no longer served me. I chose to claim it and made the decision the last day of the *Phoenix Rising* course that I was not going to allow Crohn's to claim me and run my life. I chose to claim the Crohn's, thanked it for the time I needed it and declared that it was time to move on to bigger things.

I can no longer do small things. I am more willing to go BIG with my life and I know who I am capable of becoming. I walked out of the *Phoenix Rising* course with no Crohn's, no anemia, no thalassemia, and I am no longer prone to getting phlebitis. Maybe a month after the course, I had gone to the doctor – who came to see that I was perfectly healthy. They couldn't believe that my iron was up to a normal level when for the last five years I had been at dangerously low levels. Everything had stabilized itself to within normal ranges. The doctors were typing away at their computer in shock as, of course, they thought to themselves "how could that be, if Crohn's can't be cured?" That's when I stood up thanked them and walked away – having never returned to the hospital from that day.

Interestingly enough, the moment at which I chose to stand 'at cause' in my life is the moment that my mother and I bumped heads. She would continuously up the ante with situations on trying to 'control' me. The harder she pushed, the more I became unwilling to engage in any conversation with her, as I was no longer willing to pretend or to be a victim. I was now fully awake and able to stand alone. So I did just that and I chose to stand alone. I packed my bags and took off at 7am while she was sleeping, heading for my own apartment.

We would have conversations, at times, and I would visit but the second my mother would begin to dance the old dance, I would end the conversation and say, "When you're willing to have a conversation about something other than what no longer serves me, call me back. I would love to chat with you". I also expressed to her that I quit as her daughter and that now, maybe we could create the space needed for us to become friends.

Slowly but surely, my mother came to know that she could no longer engage with me the way that she had in the past; and that I no longer needed her help. I had thanked her for that help and it was time for me to move on. For the first time not too long ago, I had the opportunity to contribute to her. She actually came to me for guidance! Seeing the impact that it has had on my life, she had become curious and chose to listen and discover more about the world that I live in. All I can say is that it opened doors.

I cannot express to you the feeling deep down inside when you know the power you have within you to create whatever it is you want to create. It's an amazing feeling, as well as a scary feeling, as you enter what you don't know you don't know. My journey continued after that day. It didn't end there. I continued to take the WEL-Systems® courses once I knew the impact they would have on myself and who I would become. I continued the *Igniting the Self* program, from there going on to *Resourcefulness in Action*, and then the Master Facilitator certification program *Influencing with Intention*.

Influencing with Intention was huge for me as it was through this process that I realized that my artwork was an open book of who I was. We were initially supposed to write a 1000 word essay on why we chose this course and for what purpose. Instead, I chose to paint whatever came to me. I handed in my painted essay and thought that was it. Little did I know that this very painting was the entire focus on why I was there and what I needed to learn about myself.

I had so much information moving through me with this painting that my whole body went into muscle spasm, leaving me no longer able to move for some moments. My arms and legs became stiff like planks of wood. My face must have been squished in because I could feel it but my eyes where closed. All I could do was laugh and cry, all at the same time. My body would not respond to my desire for movement.

I had four people from the group working with me to help me relax my body so that it could do the work of metabolizing or moving the energy/information through my whole body and be 'digested'. Slowly but surely, I was able to move my fingers and legs. Then came the time for me to walk. It felt like I actually had to learn how to walk again as my whole body had restructured and rewired itself completely, with new information that I hadn't known in my conscious awareness.

Had I been anywhere else but in that room I know I would have called an ambulance and I would have panicked. But within the experience and the space that I was willing to create for myself in allowing myself to experience this without any judgment, I also created a huge feeling of safety within myself and within that room with those people who surrounded me. I knew – deep inside myself – that I was safe.

You cannot have a more powerful, more profound experience than being willing to go big with your life and choose the big ones. The ones that you may fear the most, the ones that are stored and wired deep down in your body where no one dares to go. But choosing to go BIG, and claiming that, may be the very thing that gets your life back. You'll never know until you're willing to go there and experience it for yourself.

I know that I am no longer willing to *not* go there. I continue to grow and experience life, moment to moment to moment, as I follow my huge popcorn trail and allow it to lead me where it leads me. I know fully that I have created my life from within. I now live my life noticing the metaphors and patterns that I have created. I see the intelligence within the creation itself. We are magnificent, powerful beings… and I think it's about time we 'be' who we know we can become. Thank you, Louise, for being that huge angel that stood by my side when I looked over that edge… and I flew!

Karina Evangelista was born and raised in Montreal, Quebec, Canada. A talented and accomplished artist from a very young age, Karina began creating pieces from media such as watercolors, oils, acrylics, pencil, charcoal and markers. A graphic artist, she uses programs such as Adobe Illustrator, Adobe Photoshop and Quark Xpress to design unique and compelling images to say what words cannot, from a profound passion to create inspiring works of art. A WEL-Systems Master Facilitator, Karina continues to bloom and grow with her life experiences.

A Wake-Up Call

Dorothy Spence

January 4, 2001. I walked into my home, fleeing from the press after they caught wind that my high-profile company of which I was also CEO was going into receivership. As I stepped across the threshold of the front door, my husband, Dale, was lying horizontal on the living room couch vomiting into a bucket.

It was his 40th birthday. He had also been on morphine for a few weeks with acute neck pain. Over the past four months, his neck pain mysteriously coincided with the time period during which financial troubles in my company were surfacing. Together, we face the facts: there was no physiological reason for his neck pain; there was no surgery available to alleviate such intense pain, only drugs to dull a relentless, pulsating pain that sent shock waves throughout his entire body. In my mind's eye, I had convinced myself I had done such a great job at hiding the financial realities from him and my two young children.

Within a week, I was forced to be alone with my inner-most thoughts: I knew I had to stop as I was convinced I was on the doorstep to becoming very, very ill This reality left me numb, sad and deeply confused. Finally, I realized I had no idea who I really had become or, for that matter, who my husband and my two children were.

When did this emptiness start? How had I created such a perfect life on the outside when I was so miserable on the inside? Where was I to go from here? How could I face the outside world after such a failure?

Upon reflection, the whole buying-into-a-plan-that-wasn't-mine started with my choice of university. I had chosen to study engineering for two reasons: the guidance councillor had told me that women weren't allowed to be engineers; and I was told that I would get a "good" job. This seemed to be much better than the option of staying in my small town or getting a job as a scientist cleaning test tubes. One of the questions that I didn't consider was the implication of getting a job that paid good money...but at what cost? That theme would continue to run its course throughout my life.

The University Years

As I was going through engineering, I was steadfast in my determination to finish my degree because I made a promise to myself I was going to do it, and proving to everyone that I could seemed important at the time. In hindsight, what I was really passionate about was physics.

I remember my physics professor trying to convince me that I could be a great physicist. All I could think of was how weird physics majors were and to me, their behaviour seemed bizarre.

Now almost 25 years later, I live in a world where some of my most delightful conversations are with the same physics professor that saw this spark within me and tried his best to convince me to study with him. Today, when we get together to explore and delve deeply into all he knows about quantum physics, my former teacher and mentor invites and allows me to share my stories and evolving interest in physics and spirituality.

When I graduated from university, I started down a traditional path. I met Dale in engineering school and we married a couple of years after university. It was at that point, after numerous conversations, that Dale and I came to a mutually satisfying agreement: I was going to take the prominent position as far as our respective careers were concerned as I was then, and continue to be, the risk-taker in the family - some say an intensity junkie. Dale chose the domestic domain and agreed to be the primary one to raise our children. In that regard, Dale became a community college professor and has enjoyed working with and mentoring students for over two decades. I launched my business and engineering career in technology sales.

When I look back at our early times together, my pattern of behaviour as a seeker is evident in all the choices I have made. Especially my thirst for knowledge, new experiences of people and places, and my desire to learn to be more and more reflective.

Early on, I conceived of a plan for travelling throughout the South Pacific with Dale for four months. It was a wonderful way of expanding my world; in all honesty, a world that was feeling very confined in the traditional 9 to 5 job. From the very beginning, the two weeks vacations and the weekends were not enough for me as I had a voracious appetite to see the world and experience other cultures. I simply needed to colour outside the lines.

Thankfully, the world of technology sales continued to afford me the opportunity to travel and meet all kinds of interesting people around the globe.

A Baby Girl & A Baby Manager

When I turned 29, we decided it was time to "settle down" and start a family. I remember the day that the pharmacist told me the pregnancy test was positive. I was both thrilled and terrified. The day I gave birth to my daughter was one of the most special and scared moments of my life. I remember the awe of the miracle of life.

It also started me on the path of small boxes, more responsibility and pressures. All of these were creations in my own mind. I didn't want to be "just" a mother; I wanted more.

It was at that time that I was "promoted" in my job to become a middle level manager. I remember becoming aware of how complex it was to manage people. I had a clear analogy in my head about sales being a process similar to railway tracks and managing people like a big plate of spaghetti. The relationships were twisted together, entwined and when you pulled at one piece of spaghetti, a number of them came along. It seemed that anything I did wasn't the right thing. It was my first experience of corporate politics. I was spending over 70% of my job dealing with office/staff politics rather than getting my job done. The people issues were consuming most of my time. I remember thinking that organizations are fine until they put people into them.

I had just spent the last ten years of my life learning how to get an answer, do analysis, and determine the best course of action based on that "right" answer. No one in engineering school ever talked to me about the complexity of people. I began to discover this was going to be the most important thing for me to learn and that discovery needed to start with me first. I received no external recognition for the job I was performing, only complaints and criticism. This certainly wasn't the same as the sales environment. I had received sales awards every year and lots of external recognition. Even though my need for external validation wasn't getting any fuel, I did have a growing sense that I had an extreme interest in people and they were comfortable trusting and talking to me.

A Baby Boy and Wanderlust

Another baby and another exotic trip throughout Europe to deepen my experience of life as a seeker. However, this time there was no hitchhiking and going on treks for five days at a time because Dale and I now had a young – very young! - family. This time, we rented a car and organized accommodation in small apartments throughout Europe. I was naive in thinking that my son was going to be the same baby as my daughter; he was much more active and didn't sleep like she did in those early months of her life. It goes without saying that Dale and I were exhausted travelling around Europe with a seven week old baby and a three year old. Often I find myself wondering what could I possibly have been searching for; or worse, what was I trying to prove and to whom? What were these deep, internal desires to know more, see more and experience more all about? What motivated me to wander off around the globe both before we had children and after we had children? What was it about other cultures that drove this inner desire I called wanderlust?

When I got back from Europe, my manager informed me that the company was restructuring and offered me a severance package. I was also invited to meet the new president of the area to discuss possible job opportunities with him but his sexist attitudes towards women in management prevented any possibilities in this regard. Like many women wanting to work in management positions, I found myself being sexually harassed as a right of passage into middle management. Of course, I refused to accept that this workplace norm would affect my personal and professional life.

Leadership Styles Observed

By this time in my career, I had worked with three leaders: two men and one woman. I had started to notice some differences in the leadership style of all three. I was also starting to notice the effect of the leader on the culture of the companies that they were running. It seemed that all of the issues that couldn't get resolved were because of the leader taking a strong position on an issue and pushing for what they thought was the right answer instead of opening up to other people's ideas.

The next phase of my life consisted of a lot of intensity. I was back doing my MBA full time, my son was six months old and still not sleeping, my daughter was 3 and my husband was also back in University getting his Masters in Education.

On top of this, I decided to join a former colleague and start a consulting business. The theory was that this was going to give us flexibility and money.

My partner, Linda, was also an engineer, a young mother and a year ahead of me doing her MBA. I figured if I got my MBA, I'd be even better prepared to deal with the people issues and gain the business knowledge that I lacked. I also felt it would give me the opportunity to distinguish myself from the others in engineering and clearly demonstrate a commitment and investment in becoming a business person.

Incredibly, my husband held down the fort at home and offered me as much support as I needed. Understandably, he was hurt and upset when I would go out socializing with my classmates after class on Friday night - rather than being the traditional wife and coming home and spending quality time with my young family. However, on the other hand, Dale's inner wisdom communicated clearly that I was not a traditional wife and that was why he both loved and supported me on all my quests.

That was a pattern that I maintained for the next seven years. It was a very lonely time for my husband. He watched me disconnect from my self, from him and from my young children. He stepped in to be both the mother and father.

The Entrepreneurial Years

The company that Linda and I co-founded grew very rapidly during our first year in business. We had evolved the company from a health care technology consulting practice into a telehealth technology company. We had revenue of over $1M in our first year and we were profitable. For some reason, I started doubting that we could do this alone. We had put second mortgages on our homes and we needed some outside advisors. What was interesting about the partnership was that we were both "weird ducks" in the corporate world and we were making up all of our own rules and, interestingly, they

A Wake-Up Call

were working. The way that we engaged our employees was real; we had a lot of laughter and a sense that we could take on the world. My role was one where I continued to be plagued with the growth issues that I thought were on the horizon. I went out and found our first investor and strategic partner.

On my health side, I gained forty pounds within 6 months of getting the outside investor into the company. I was becoming increasingly uncomfortable with the way decisions were getting made. The CEO of the company who invested in us started training me as a traditional CEO. The Board of Directors of our company was not a reflection of who Linda and I were, but of a more traditional board structure. At some point, the meaning of the business and the magic of creating something different became lost in the quest to make money. Also lost was the original idea of creating a company that treated people differently. I'm not saying the investors did this to me, rather I allowed this to happen.

I remember being at an awards ceremony and they were introducing Linda and me. I was thinking that they were talking about someone outside of the real me. I felt that there was the public me and the private me. I was in a disassociated state most of the time. I felt like it was a scam; deep down I felt I had tricked everyone, including myself.

By this time, the company was flourishing. I was travelling around the world, doing business in places as exotic as Kuwait and the Caribbean. We had offices across Canada and 45 people on payroll. We had investors and write-ups in the most prestigious magazines, including <u>Wired</u>. Our telehealth networks were growing and I was dying inside.

In the midst of transitioning the company towards a new business model, my business partner and I got caught in the perfect storm. The market had disappeared as the funding for these projects went from provincial to federal money with a 3 year time lag. The technology bubble had burst and our financing to take the company public had fallen through. All of these events happened within four months. Both Linda and

I did a lot of soul searching and decided that neither one of us had enough "fire" in our bellies to continue on. We knew that by putting the company into receivership, the essence of the magic that we had created would be maintained.

The Journey Within

This was a turning point --- the still point in my life journey. I took a long break to make sure I took care of myself first. I remember my daughter, who was 10 at the time, being quite honest and telling me she didn't want me coming in and out of her life. She would prefer I was either in or out. My son was very happy to have me in his life as he hadn't experienced that before. My husband was scared, tired and confused. I started what has become known in our family as my "inner journey". It started with little things that broke my traditional pattern. As an example, I took saxophone lessons because I always wanted to play the sax but felt like I never had time. I took over running the household. That was a very difficult set of tasks for me to take over and ones that, still today, are very conflicted. Even though I want my home to be clean and I want to create beauty in my physical environment, I do not want to be the one doing the housework. This still remains a flash point amongst all family members.

There were a number of people who showed up for me on this path who extended a warm heart and helping hand. I will never forget the kindness and help that was offered. Yet I knew that I needed to walk this path by myself. It was really hard and ugly at first. I had a lot to face including the potential of personal bankruptcy, poor health and very little connection with my family. Yet I knew that I had to do this in order to fill the emptiness inside of myself.

Energy as Information

One of the people that inspired me was a friend of mine, Cathy. She was over 60 years old and had the laughter and vitality of someone so much younger than me. I didn't know exactly what it was that she had but I knew whatever it was, I wanted some. I started working with her as a business coach. It was so interesting because she started providing me with information and a worldview I hadn't known of before. She seemed so mystical, spiritual and loving. Cathy was able to teach me how to reconnect with myself and to use my body as a processor of information. Most of what she told me was intriguing and what I considered weird or way out there. Engineers are not known for their tendency to be "way out there." I also felt compelled to continue along the path she was showing me as I was getting significant results.

I clearly remember one day we were talking about a situation at work. It seemed like I was always in battle with my peers which may beg a question about how I view competitive situations. She encouraged me to view my work situations as a metaphor and we started to explore why I felt like I was competing against other people. She showed me how to go inside of my body and access the information and energy that was stored in my body. She helped me understand how my body could process that information rather than have my intellect label it as an emotion. A wave moved through my body and I opened my eyes. I couldn't believe that it was that easy.

Sure enough, the next day, while in conversation with my peer, I noticed I wasn't competing against him anymore. There was nothing to struggle against. It was one of the few times I had experienced my crucible energy. Instead of my experience being like that of those business leaders who would hit a wall, I softened, slowed down and experienced another person a completely different way. I started to realize that I could change and that the change could help me become who I was (or my authentic self) rather than someone I thought I should be. And it was so easy and fast.

Waking Up

I knew there had to be a different way to approach life and I knew that I had the courage to take that journey. I wanted a life of meaning and abundance. I wanted it to be shaped consciously by what I wanted for myself rather than what others thought I'd be good at. I wanted to live a life based on my unique purpose and intention. I wanted to be drawn towards something rather than run away from being a victim.

I also felt that there was a way to provide leadership within organizations that was not based on the traditional models. These organizations focused on people development. Even though I had joked about it early in my career, it was becoming more and more obvious that leaders who created transformational work environments were growing their companies faster and more profitably than the others. Throughout my entire career, I had been attracted to work environments where the leader of the company ran the organization based on a command-and-control model rather than a new, fresh way of looking at leadership. I knew that it would be in combining the revelation of my inner truth, the creation of open systems and open expression of what was really going on that a difference would be made.

I realized that to do the deep inner work that I felt I needed, I would have to make a significant investment in myself. This seemed like a difficult task. Hadn't I put my family through enough hardship? When I started taking programs through the WEL-Systems® Institute, I catalyzed the process. For a year and a half I read, studied and created the space to understand myself from the inside out. I knew this was needed in order to interrupt the tapes inside of my head and the habits that seemed to run on auto pilot and ran my life.

One of these patterns that I became aware of was the family hero strategy that I ran and had great success with. What this meant was I felt like I had to be responsible for everyone and everything that was happening to them. I felt it was my job to make everything better. That became extremely tiring when I had a lot of employees and a family at home. This was an intelligent response that became wired in during my childhood. What I discovered is that it made me tired and it also enabled other people to depend on me rather than do their own thing. An example of this was viewing the receivership of my first company as something that I was fully responsible for. I didn't view this as a shared responsibility of the board of directors and my business partner. I have since been in situations where I have noticed that I do not engage in what I affectionately call the "blame game" and certainly do not feel like every adverse event is my sole responsibility.

I have learned to stay in the question rather than feeling compelled to not only have the answer, but the right answer. This has been a particularly difficult behaviour for me to learn. I had been trained as an engineer and rewarded throughout my career to have the answer. I had to learn to relax into not knowing. This was at first very uncomfortable and I felt a lot of pressure from the inside to move. After all, my entire life I had been rewarded based on knowing! I learned to relax and see where life took me. And it has taken me to wonderful and completely different places from any I could have ever imagined.

My beliefs about time and money have been shifted completely. I used to believe that I needed to do certain jobs to make a certain amount of money and then I would be happy. When that didn't happen, I started to dig into my culturally conditioned beliefs to see what was underneath. I became aware of how judgemental I was based on a person's income and wealth. This really surprised me as I never really felt like I was prejudiced in this regard. I began to notice people around me who had a sense of adventure and joy in their lives rather than burden and drudgery. I noticed a pattern that people who do what they are passionate about seemed to have a lightness about them. I have now shifted my belief about money to be more a reflection about doing work that you are passionate about. When I hear people talking about being in it for the money, I can now see more of the boundaries they have allowed to have around themselves. I have also begun to explore a lot of my beliefs about time. I have noticed how I viewed time as scarce. I no longer wear a watch and I have freed myself from the majority of time constraints that I used to put around myself in relation to time. All of those boundaries and restrictions I created in my own mind, for an abstract concept that is not absolute and was instead something that we created in order to help me label and construct boundaries.

Who have I become as a result of this inner journey?

I have become a whole person and I continuously strive to become my authentic self. When my body speaks, I listen. My days tend to flow instead of bracing and pushing against them. I am compelled forward by my intention in life, my unique reason for being and what I have to contribute that no one else on the face of this earth can because they have not had my experiences. This state of being provides for a completely different way for me to move through my world, rather than continue from my previous history of trying to prove something and running away from being who I didn't want to be. My new path is a much more peaceful state that provides me with clarity and focus. It allows me to be more open to new information and accepting of other people's ideas. It has made me much more compassionate and has enriched my sense of humour enormously. I spend much more of my energy being present to what is occurring in my everyday life instead of planning six to 12 months ahead. I have begun the process of noticing the boundaries and the limitations that I put around events.

An Infinite Game

I have discovered what it feels like when I notice the boundaries and then start to play with them. Through this process I have discovered what an infinite game feels like. My infinite game is life. It's enjoying the small things in the ordinary of the everyday experience of life. A recent example of this was the way I viewed a situation that happened to me while I was out of the country on training. The night before the training started, I received a 3:00 a.m. and 5:30 a.m. wake up call from the front desk. In the past, I would have been irritated about it all day, and noticed how tired I was, and stayed in a victim position throughout the day. The conversation would have been all about what someone did to me. Instead, I chose to view it as a metaphor that I had created to tell myself something. The message I chose to take from this was to wake up and to pay attention to what was going on with the training. What a delightful and different way for me to approach the day. I had a wonderful day and I learned all kinds of things about myself.

I have discovered that as I have created change within me, I have become the invitation for growth in others. My children, who are now both teenagers, have engaged in a process of doing what they want instead of doing what others think they should do. My daughter has completely changed her high school courses to be a reflection of her interests rather than her parents' thoughts or beliefs.

Growth Matters

I hold a belief that growth is a biological imperative. A cell can either be in growth or protection and not both at the same time. I have become much more aware of physical and energetic manifestations of growth (abundance) and protection (scarcity) all the time. As an example, I have noticed that when I start an internal conversation with myself about why I can't do something, I become aware of the conversation and ask: "why am I limiting myself in this way"? I have found that the reason, in the majority of cases, is that I am trying to protect some belief that I have held about myself in the past. For example, one common one for me is that I can't stick my neck out. I have had many situations in the past where sticking my neck out was a very dangerous thing to do. I have been ridiculed, emotionally beaten up and silenced in the past.

And yet, I now know that pushing the edge of self discovery requires me to reveal myself and stick my neck out. Although it always involves a risk, I view it as a gift; and know that by proceeding and going to places where I am very uncomfortable, I am going to be experiencing something new for me that allows me to grow --- as a person, a professional and, ultimately, a growth leader. My true definition of the infinite game I call my life is to be clear about one thing: that is, growth!

Dorothy Spence - P.Eng. MBA, WEL-Systems® Catalyst and CODE Model Coach™ - of Growth Matters Inc. is a growth leader working with CEOs of cutting-edge companies. With many years of founding and evolving early stage technology companies, Dorothy enjoys playing a catalytic role in growth initiatives within companies. She particularly enjoys inviting conversations that accelerate leadership and personal growth.

A Wake-Up Call

Bursting Into Flame

Eva Marsh

My Fire has always yearned to burst into a huge flame!

One of my earliest memories is being harnessed for a walk with my parents. They didn't want me to fall down and hurt myself. I grew up restless for space to flex and explore without constriction. I slept between my teenage cousins who told me not to move around so much. My mother said her boyfriend was a neighbour or my imagination, and the summer I was eight curious physical symptoms became evident.

Sometimes when I played tag my right knee would buckle and the other kids would laugh loudly as I lay in a heap on the grass. I had difficulty in determining my left from right. This made gym periods agony and I pretended that I didn't care about organized sports because the teasing was vicious. My father thought I was clumsy, and decided that ballet lessons might help me to be more graceful.

In the airy studio, and at home in the basement, I had space to spin and leap for hours. Dancing was freedom to think and move without disapproval. I also loved going to school and learning new things but my marks led to bullying by classmates.

I felt hot and cold prickles all over my body. The teachers would tell me to "sit still" while my parents would tell me to run around outside and work off all that energy. My mother said her boyfriend was the taxi driver... or my imagination... and at 16, in the cold days of January, I lost my sight.

There was a round of doctors' appointments where not much was said. One specialist told me that I had experienced paralysis of the optic nerve. He said it would be several weeks before my eyes were back to normal - and it might happen again. Next time, perhaps an arm or a leg could be involved, but it would always go away in time. Mostly I was sad that my parents believed it was just my imagination. They never spoke with the doctor and I was left to my own devices.

Everything was grey and green (like an underwater movie!) as I made my way around the yard with my dog. When my sight began to return, we set off to explore the open fields and by September, my sight was fully restored.

I stayed with relatives while I finished high school, and was shocked that the world could be so different 300 miles away. For the first time, I had to do things for myself, like make a purchase and pay a cashier. It was terrifying to take responsibility for me with no prior warning.

Although my marks dropped, I was awarded a bursary for college. This too, was a very different world with no rules to guide a naive convent-trained student. My parents thought more education was a waste because "girls get married and husbands support them."

After first year, I was married, pregnant and working full-time in a pharmacology research laboratory. I continued to experience the odd bizarre symptom, explained away by the family doctor as just a whimsy.

One morning in March 1967, I was unable to move when I woke up. It didn't take doctors long to guess the diagnosis. Suddenly, two words made me a stranger. Multiple Sclerosis. My husband stared at his hands, picking his nails. In his mind these two words stripped me of my individuality and guaranteed a life with no future. I could sense the fear and revulsion in a cloud around him.

A Wake-Up Call

I was only 22 years old. I hadn't even lived yet. How could we be talking about dying? Time stopped; there was nothing but a void where our lives had been. I couldn't think what to do, so I sat.

The next morning he prepared to leave for classes, pretending to be surprised that I had been sitting all night. I hadn't moved in 12 hours. No one expected me to be able to do anything.

I came back from my safe spot in the corner of the ceiling and rallied with the implicit 'knowing' that I had to be here. No one else was qualified to raise my girls. They were two and one year old; already their own ambitious personalities and I was determined their lives would not be spoiled by my problem.

My next conscious thought was the need for facts and I asked my husband to bring me information from the medical library. One leg was paralysed and the other had no sensation. My eyes jerked annoyingly to one side. When I stood in front of the mirror, I looked the same as I did yesterday and my legal identification was still valid, but everything about me was changed and nothing would ever be the same.

One doctor had told me that too much physical activity and stress would accelerate the progress of the disease. He had assured me that there wouldn't be any pain because the nerves die. I exploded when he said 'they' were doing very good research, and that when I accepted 'it,' I'd be more realistic. Acceptance implies a choice. What choice? Quit and die, or fight and die? Not only had I been changed, but my reality was being redefined in terms that I didn't understand. How could I accept what I didn't understand?

That evening, I read words in the medical books about disability and death but there was nothing to tell me what I needed to know to live. Virus, autoimmunity, carbohydrate metabolism, unnamed enzymes, serum albumin deficiencies - these were all just hypotheses as to the cause of MS. It's all a guessing game, so how could anyone be so sure that my life was over? What about getting functions back? The body repairs all kinds of damage; it doesn't make sense that damaged nerves can't repair in some way.

A few weeks ago my legs had been very bad, but now there was an improvement. I couldn't stay in bed. The daily household routine had to be carried out. If I didn't keep trying to make my legs work, I'd never know if there had been some repair.

I believed that my husband was the strongest person I had ever met. If his reaction was to avoid me, how would my family and friends react? I couldn't cope with more rejection - I didn't want to be alone. If people would stay away from me because I had MS, I decided I wouldn't tell anyone. I'd pretend that everything was fine. I wouldn't talk about the specialists and the diagnosis. Somehow I'd bluff it through. When we played bridge and I bid my hands too high, my partner always said, "Play 'em like ya got 'em, Eve." I'd play all right. I'd bluff for the life of me.

For final confirmation of the diagnosis, I kept an appointment with a neurologist who had followed more than four hundred cases of MS in his career. No two had progressed in the same way; some people had gotten along for years with few problems, and others had progressed very quickly to wheelchairs and beds. He had also seen many cases with long remissions between episodes. No one really could say what the prognosis would be.

He believed that a personality factor must be considered because those people who keep up their spirits and stay busy, did much better than others. I thought my husband would be encouraged by this neurologist's experience, but all that he heard was that the diagnosis had been confirmed. The rest, he said, was just to shut me up. He had news of his own: a summer job in Prince Edward Island. His frat brothers needed him there. He owed them.

A Wake-Up Call

Determined to keep up appearances like a good wife should, I tried to keep my marriage together, even at the cost of my dignity and self-respect. Divorce was a sin and I kept fooling myself that everything would be all right. I persuaded myself the summer would give him time to sort things out in his own mind, and with his return in September, I was sure that our marriage would be stronger. He just needed more time.

The summer gave me space and time to figure out what I needed to do. The prospect of being on my own with the children wasn't frightening anymore. It was another challenge in my life, and the first test of my intention to live as normally as possible.

In June, when I could easily drive the Volkswagen again, I returned to work in the lab. Summer left the campus deserted and I was always alone, even in the lab. There were fewer experiments to do, so I had more time to read and study. Besides sending for reprints of articles relevant to my job, I also requested articles about multiple sclerosis. I was curious to know what happened in the nervous system. The difference between research studies and articles printed in research journals quickly became evident; publication was often justified in spite of considerable gaps in information. I became dismayed by exaggerated theories with statistical gamesmanship and no evidence.

In the 1966 volume of the journal *Neurology*, I found an article titled *"Regeneration of myelin in multiple sclerosis,"* by Feigin and Popoff. By studying slides of tissue with an electron microscope, they found evidence of myelin repair in MS plaques of damage. The newly formed myelin was not identical to the original myelin. So what? It must do the job, after all I was walking again, and driving, and climbing stairs. There must have been enough repair to allow me to function as before.

The paper concluded that if ways were found to enhance the regeneration observed in this study, a clinically useful purpose might be served. Did I enhance the process by making myself resume my regular activities? Was it that simple? Did the girls enhance the process by expecting me to go on as usual? They didn't pay attention to my right leg that scuffed or my right knee that didn't bend properly. So I didn't either, and soon my walk was normal again.

Another interesting paper by Bunge, Bunge and Ris, 1961, described the first sign of myelin repair 19 days after damage; by 64 days all damage was thinly repaired. The authors suggested that myelin is reformed in the same way it is first formed in normal development, but note that this didn't agree with accepted opinion. I was encouraged because advances are not made by people who think the same as everybody else.

Another observation stood out:

> "The neurological condition of the experimental animal begins to improve at a time when remyelination begins and has returned to normal by the time most axons are at least partly remyelinated."

I was sure that all these kitty-cats wanted to get going as soon as possible. They did it in 64 days, and it took me from March to the middle of May. Purrty close.

I was driven to better comprehend the research I had found. The process of restoring damaged myelin is similar to the normal process of myelin development as the nervous system matures. This view did not agree with generally held views and I felt in harmony because I did not agree with views held about the prognosis for MS.

In an embryology text, I read that myelin forms in response to demand. I had watched the normal development of my babies as they learned to crawl and walk in response to their instinct for movement. They didn't think about it or analyse it, they just did it. My instincts were to look after my family and get back to work, and from the time of the diagnosis in March until I resumed my duties in the lab in June, my progress back to normal was continuous.

A Wake-Up Call

My excitement at making the connection was palpable. Science was supporting my intuition. Not only did it explain my recovery, it also gave me assurance that I would always recover. There was no need to fear the future course of ms. So I began to pay attention to looking as healthy as I felt. After I cut my hair and shampooed in some highlights, I tackled my wardrobe. I had never thought about mortality before, or how I could make my life count. If all that I can give to the people I care about is memories, I want them to be pleasant ones.

Suddenly it was graduation day and we moved to the West, my husband's home. My in-laws were slow to accept me because I was a despised Easterner, and they had expected him to marry a nice Western girl. Despite my misgivings, we moved to a house on the family ranch property. From every direction, I could look at the prairie and watch the cattle grazing, celebrate the morning sky and the heart-wrenching sunsets.

The expanded operation of the ranch took all the energy that my husband had. When he wasn't working, he was sleeping in exhaustion. He didn't have time to accept any invitations to socialize. The neighbours were cordial but their suspicion of outsiders, especially Easterners, meant that few offers to "Drop in for coffee" were forthcoming.

By mid-September my right arm was becoming clumsy and weak and there was a loss of sensation in my legs. My chest felt tight, and for a while being active kept my mind off the significance of these changes. The doctor tested my reflexes and said uneasily that it was a good thing that I wasn't a violinist. When I pressed him to suggest something more medical, he told me to stop at the liquor store on my way home. I had never thought of playing the violin.

My husband pointed out an article about a Russian vaccine for MS in a farm publication from the Food and Drug Directorate. He told me not to get my hopes up, not to be gullible just because it said 'research'. He said that many people think they have nothing to lose ... there might be a chance ... but the greatest chance with this stuff in the research stage is harmful side effects, wrong doses or just plain bad research.

From his experience in college, he knew that people publish anything to keep their jobs, to get more grant money, to save reputations by trying to validate poor work. He told me not to be naive, that research was just another business. Not all researchers do good, honest work. The more definite they are, the more suspicious you have to be. They pretend to be certain even when there is no certainty about the cause, the treatment or even the diagnosis!

The disillusion was too much to bear. A joking doctor and a joke for research. I was too disheartened to read the article carefully, but I noted that Canada has refused entry of the vaccine, "in the best interests of the Canadian public." I didn't want to think about it anymore.

More and more nights I was alone again. There was business in town. My condition continued to deteriorate and it was hard to contend with the double vision that made walking even more hazardous. I covered one eye when I read to my girls.

The family doctor told me that I don't have long, so I should get ready for 'IT'. All the chemicals are turning me into a zombie and I wanted to stop all the drugs, but he refused to discontinue my medication. I flushed the sleeping pills and tranquillizers down the toilet. My energy returned, and my head cleared enough to see that all the drugs rendered me almost incompetent. But I was expected to carry out my maternal obligation without bothering the family or any of the neighbours, even though my husband left to help yet another frat brother.

In October, I blindly picked a neurologist out of the city phone book and by December there was a bed available at the hospital. The specialist's confidence in the latest drug inspired me with the trust to ignore what I had seen in medical

A Wake-Up Call

journals where studies seemed to prove that drug treatments for multiple sclerosis were ineffective. The days melted away in a druggy haze and the doctor was annoyed with me for not walking more. Even though I knew I should get up, I just had no ambition to move or read or even to think.

One day, the physiotherapist directed me to sit in front of the mirror to retrain the body position sensors to maintain my posture correctly. After several tries, I understood that I needed to remind my body how to hold itself up correctly. With physio, I could feel my legs getting stronger and I knew that I'd have no problems keeping up the routine.

Once home, the marriage quickly folded. Custody of the children wasn't an issue - he was certain he'd have the children back soon. I kept my mouth shut. On the train, I sat facing east and formed the intention to make a new life for myself and my girls. It didn't matter that I didn't have a clue how it would happen. The Fire was beginning to awaken.

One day at a time, I focussed attention on my children and creating a new life. My parents made numerous comments about my laziness when I didn't look for a job, so I told them about the diagnosis. They were prepared to look after me because it was their obligation as parents. My obligation was to be passive, and give up control. My Father bristled when I said I'd look after my own bills and handle my own money. I had no intention of letting mySelf be harnessed again.

No one expected me to survive on my own, so I had the space to do things my way. After school and on the weekends, the girls and I prowled the city finding the parks and pools. Even when the fall winds turned raw, we bundled up and went to the lakeshore to be soothed by the water and wind. I began to feel rooted.

Every day, I did yoga with the lady on TV. My head was clearer and I was less fatigued. My movements were not as stiff and awkward. As I increased my control over my limbs, breathing calmed my mind and I gained in confidence. Now as I moved into the chaos of life, I would breathe deeply and relax my body. Life improved.

That this amazing philosophy had endured for thousands of years fascinated me. I read book after book to feed my hunger to find a way to peace and self-fulfilment. I was intrigued by the concept of a universal source of energy.

With this space, I was able to confront the memories that crowded my mind when I lay down to sleep. I recognized that a part of me wanted to keep the hurts fresh and the anger hot. Deep breathing and relaxation exercises helped me to let go of the day and fall asleep.

I became aware how my upbringing had conditioned me to many confusing values and a bias in attitude. The power in letting go of beliefs that no longer served me, indeed if they ever had, strengthened my mind, body and spirit. Although there were more episodes of symptoms, the girls and I created a flow of pleasant days and relaxed evenings, and I always recovered.

In spite of assurances by doctors that I had too much brain damage, I decided to complete my university education. I planned to begin with one course and gauge what load I could carry without jeopardizing my health. The registrar didn't refer to my medical history.

After first year, I decided the only sensible course was to proceed with the study of physics to better understand events at the quantum level in the nervous system. I was curious … was the mechanism that encouraged repair in the nervous system as basic as the demand of the nervous system for feedback and response? By volunteering my time to work on an interesting neuromuscular research project, I learned as collaborator - not as subject.

A Wake-Up Call

It was fascinating to learn that quantum physics doesn't describe the real world but describes the probability that the possibility chosen by the observer will manifest as reality. Applied to multiple sclerosis, this suggests that the 'reality' of ms is the possibility chosen by the observer.

With my recent introduction to the genius of WEL-Systems® models, I see how my progress through life can be understood in terms of an Open Loop System™. Time and again, in the context of my evolution, I was flung into a space where dysfunctional beliefs about my Self, family, marriage and religion collapsed; where this space made room for movement and change, to create the reality I desired.

Choosing to hold a clear intention was paramount in my evolution. The intention to raise my children, to build a new life and the intention to excel in university all became reality because I trusted my body to heal, my mind to learn and my Self to define reality. Everything else fell into place.

For the world around me, I am a model of healing and recovery. From the world around me, I attract others who see me as a resource for information and ideas for reclaiming the Fire within themselves. I continue to explore the metaphor of MS as an expression of constriction, paralysis, insensibility, numbness and the suspension of reality in life. And as the loop opens for the next stage of my evolution, I am ready to move on. In the past, I wanted to leave people with present memories. In the present, I am coaching others to create exciting futures.

More people are drawn to investigate, as those who experience The CODE Model™ and Quantum TLC™ in coaching sessions share their experiences. I feel my Fire blaze as they learn to work with their bodies. When energy flows easily, the body is well.

During my recent trip to Kuwait, I shared my experience of recovery in the context of the WEL-Systems® perspective that points out new gateways to expand the Genius of our human potential. The response resulted in an invitation to return to share more. Louise has offered to work with me to prepare a two day experience introducing the WEL-Systems Body of Knowledge and the invitation to **T**rigger **L**ife **C**hoices for creation of the reality each of us desires. It is exciting to be a fractal of the WEL-Systems movement to 'spread the word' to the world. At home, I have put a new warp on my loom to satisfy a deep need to weave new creations.

Researcher, author, speaker, specializing in recovery from neurological disorders. Eva Marsh has experienced the symptoms of multiple sclerosis since the age of eight. She found research to explain her recovery, and with the review of research that began 40 years ago, challenges accepted opinions. As a Certified WEL-Systems® Catalyst and CODE Model Coach™, Eva is committed to giving back to the world with talks and workshops on life altering changes as she continues to create new ways to support others in their own evolution.

A Wake-Up Call

Moments in an Indian Girl's Life

Harjit Shokar

'When sleeping women wake, mountains move.'

~Chinese Proverb

This is a story of my awakening of the Fire I have held within myself.

I am an East Indian woman who was born in England to Indian parents who had immigrated to England from India. There are many beliefs I carry about the Indian culture based on my experience and the experiences of others that I have observed. As in all cultures, there is a wide spectrum on which it operates. What I describe here is not all encompassing but a certain point on the spectrum which I have seen; an aspect that I do not wish to ignore but wish to explore with others who have also seen or experienced this side.

I would say that ours is a culture like many others where males play a dominant role. It is very important for the line of male heirs to be established, such that the birth of sons is celebrated. When a daughter is born, in many households this would be received as if a death had occurred. Our culture is also known for female infanticide. Although it does not occur as frequently in Western countries, this is especially true in countries like India.

A son and daughter of one family can lead very different lives. Males are revered in society for their strength and abilities. They are considered to be bringers of good luck, wealth and status to a family. Daughters in many families are considered as unlucky. They are a burden on the family and they are never truly accepted as belonging to that family. It is always said that a daughter's real home is that of her husband's. So they almost come into the world as orphans.

The question of whether this is right or wrong can only be answered by each individual. There are many women who wholeheartedly believe in a system of giving deference to and placing a higher value on males, so it would be unfair to say that the culture is full of oppressed women who are under the thumb. If they truly believe their place is lower than that of the male members of their family and they are happy with this then no one can say that any atrocity is being done. Many generations of women in our culture do in fact carry such beliefs. It is what they have learned from their parents and, in turn, their parents have learned from theirs. However, we are seeing a change in the new generations.

There is an awakening of sorts going on in our culture, where young women are no longer content to have their lives be run by men. They are no longer content to have their worth measured against that of men. Even with these new beliefs, though, it is hard for such women to break out of the only world they know. For some, it seems a giant leap to actually take their beliefs and act on them at the risk of losing all they have. This story is for those women who dream of making that leap, and to know that it is possible.

I was the second girl born into a family where the hope was always for a male. You can imagine the celebration of food and drink that went on that night… NOT!!! Ah, my poor parents! Their worries wouldn't end with me. There would be one more girl after me before I suppose they'd had enough. Were we loved? Even though as a child there were times you wouldn't know it; and maybe it wasn't always clearly shown, I know now that yes, indeed, we were loved and still are today. However, our gender played a definitive role in the way we were raised and it contributed to the beliefs that were ingrained in us and that would, in turn, impact our lives as women.

I believe my parents did the best job they knew how to do as parents, based on the conditions under which they grew up in. And it is always a parent's dream to give their children what they never had and I believe they accomplished this as well. However, speaking for myself, I always felt unease with all the rules and beliefs that I was taught about my role as a female. Now this didn't have to be something someone sat down and told me, it was blatantly clear all around in the environment.

So what was it like growing up for me... well I don't actually remember a lot, but the word SCARY comes to mind. Yup that would sum a lot of it up. From a very early age I understood that there was a dangerous world out there, especially for girls.

I didn't have to get hit to fear my parents. No, in our house you would be shit scared of just a look! My mum could make those eyes of hers bore into your very soul such that you would be paralyzed with fear. She still tries it today sometimes, but either she's lost her touch or I just know better because all it evokes in me today is laughter. I just have to ask her 'Mum is there something you want to say to me?' But back then she had the power.

So, like I said, it wasn't all about being hit, not that I wasn't hit. Oh, there are some memorable times of that too. And you know what? If the boys would be hit just as much as the girls and for the same reason, I don't think I would have any issue with it. But the fact was that girls were just made out of a different sort of stuff, I suppose; and boys are so precious you don't actually want to kill them but girls are a dispensable commodity. Right! Yes I suppose some would say I exaggerate here but it is my truth.

There was so much fear in my young life that thinking back, I sort of lived in a warped world. It is hard to explain and expand on so much, in a few pages, so the best way for you to have a glimpse into me is if I tell you some memorable bits and bobs; those that I have carried with me and which undoubtedly have had a profound effect on my life.

Socializing with friends was not allowed. I wasn't able to go play at my friend's house which in turn affected the extent to which I could bond with my friends at school. Many of them would be going to each other's houses and they also were of the same culture as me. But one day, to my surprise, I was not only invited to my friend's birthday party but my mum actually said I could go. Now this was going to be my first party. I believe I was about eight years old. Oh, by the way, if you haven't guessed already, friends were female only. Socializing with boys would get you shot!

So a gift and card were bought and I was told that I had to be home by a certain time. I believe it was something like an hour and a half. As this was my first party, I had no idea about what goes on. I just thought you go in, have cake, come home - so an hour and a half seemed like more than enough time for me. When I got there, I was surprised at the kindness and love that my friend's mother (let's call her Suzy) gave to me. They certainly were wealthier than we were, so maybe that's why they seemed so loving, especially towards their daughter - *a girl*! There was something different going on in this Indian family, and I liked it.

Not everyone had arrived yet and so we all sat there, chatting and playing music and games. But as time ticked away and, being the innocent little dumb girl I was, I kept thinking to myself: when is the party supposed to start? - not knowing that this was it. Suzy's mum would pop in now and then, hugging her daughter and giving us all gentle motherly looks. I didn't even notice the time pass by until I saw the table being set up with food and the glorious cake. Now *this* is what I'd been waiting for!

Looking towards the clock, I saw that I had about 10 minutes left before my curfew. I didn't know what to do….well that's a lie. I knew I better get my ass home now, no matter what! So I thought fast. I didn't want to embarrass myself in front of all the girls and say I'm not allowed to stay, so I told Suzy's mother that I had to leave because my family was going on an outing today and unfortunately I had to go home now. Suzy's mum was shocked to say the least and she kept saying, "Of course you can stay a bit longer. Why, we are going cut the cake! Let me call your mum and explain you will be a bit late."

I thought my heart was going to burst out of my chest when she said that. NO, NO ,NO - you can't call my mother. She'll kill me! She'll say I had been disobedient, ungrateful, and that I had asked Suzy's mother to call on purpose so I could stay longer. I would really be in deep shit. I just couldn't have that happen, and I think Suzy's mum understood from my physical reaction that I really was not willing to stay. I remember the look of pity on her face, but all I cared about was getting home.

I ran all the way home and was greeted at the door by my mum who was beaming. The whole family seemed pleased that they had allowed their daughter to go to a party and she had come back in time. They had a sense of pride that they had done this for me and now they wanted me to tell them a story of what a wonderful experience they had *allowed* me to have.

Out of fear of disappointing and wanting to end this special event on a good note, I made up a big story of the party from the start to finish. "I ate lots of different things. There were chicken fingers, fries, pastries and the cake of course." Ok, so everyone was happy this had all turned out well. And I was just so glad to be home on time even though I wondered what all the girls would be doing now, probably eating cake and taking pictures. But I was safe now and that's what counted! Considering that I have very few memories, it is interesting how things I do remember are crystal clear and even today they create movement in my body.

So I didn't have much of a social life. I was pretty quiet at school, heavily into my studies. Getting good marks was very important in our family, so I studied out of fear, and actually got excellent marks. Even at home, if you were caught playing or reading a novel, my parents would ask us if we didn't have anything useful to do like school work. They used to tell me to ask my teacher for more work because I don't have enough to do....yeah right, like I'm going to go do that.

Math was a big thing in our house, as it seems to be in many Indian households. I mean seriously, you'd think Math was the answer to world peace or something - that's how much it was valued. My parents would give me extra math questions to do at home which they would then mark; and we would recite our times-tables like other kids might recite the bible, I guess! So my early years were spent being on my own really, and the one thing I did have a passion for was my studies.

There was also a lot of stress at school, as well, since it was hard to maintain the web of lies of why you were not participating in after school events; why you didn't hang out with the rest of your friends. And surely, those that I did consider friends would eventually grow apart as they wanted more than I could give. So when the opportunity to move to Canada arose, I was all for it. I had no strong attachments to friends and I wanted to escape this world of lies I had created. Canada would be a new start for me.

I was about fifteen years old when we emigrated from England to Canada, and I had a bit of a culture shock when I began school. It was almost like I was entering an American T.V. show. The kids here were so different. There was no school uniform - they seemed more into wearing what's in, having the right shoes, carrying around walkmans. I had to buy some new clothes to fit in, and that was hard when you're not even allowed to wear jeans! The first time I asked to get a walkman, I got a good swearing at, and told to mind myself. Eventually as time passed by, I would slowly be able to wear jeans and get that walkman but it took some time and some growing up - and some working on my parents.

So as we became accustomed to Canadian life, my parents also became more open. I'm sure they were concerned that we should fit in as well and maybe this was a reminder to them about the first time they immigrated to England. It seemed things were improving. But the old beliefs, values and attitudes always remained and there were many times we would be reminded of our place in this culture, and how different it was for males.

What would really be a slap in the face was when we saw our parents go shopping for a portable CD player for a six-year-old male cousin. This is something that we, as girls, were forbidden to have in our teens, let alone at that age. Our protestations stating this fact were not well received. We would be called jealous and ungrateful, along with a number of other choice words; and they clearly didn't understand how we could be hurt by their actions. They also didn't understand why we did not see how special males were in our family and how they deserved special attention. Moments like these were especially hurtful. No matter how many hurdles you felt you had crossed, there was no changing the underlying cultural beliefs.

The next big change in my life came in my early 20's. Now this is the beginning of a very worrisome time for parents of daughters in our culture. It is time to find a husband for daughters; a time to pass on the responsibility of daughters into the capable hands of a man who will now take care of them.

Here's what I have experienced of arranged marriages. The girl and her family are considered to be surfs; the boy's side are the lords. The boy's family looks at a girl's skills i.e. can she cook, clean, sew? Is she educated? As well, is she level-headed; not too opinionated? Is she controllable? Is she willing to move to live with her husband and his parents? Of course, if a good Indian family has raised their daughter right, she is all that. She is being groomed for her marriage since the day she was born. And of course, she is pure. She has not been allowed to even look towards a boy, let alone speak to one.

So now that it was time for marriage, I was supposed to be able to speak to a man, make eye-contact, be witty with him, have social conversation, and even be prepared to consummate a marriage with him… HUH?!. That equation just doesn't add up (*and I'm good at Math!*). If you are trained to stay away from men all your life and you are taught that they are dangerous, how now are you supposed to try getting one interested enough in marrying you?

I might as well have become a lesbian! I mean, I was in my mid 20's when I was doing my Master's degree, and I was working on a project with another boy in my class. And considering there were only 3 girls in a program of 23 people, it was inevitable that I got partnered with a boy. Well, he calls me on a Saturday to talk about the project and we agreed to meet at the University. That day I was accused of having a relationship with this guy and believe me! - things weren't pretty around the house.

Considering that I really didn't know of any girls who were, lets say, as *innocent* as I was at that age, I was so hurt by the accusation. After all these years, hadn't I lived up to their standards? Couldn't they trust me? And didn't they know that I still held so much fear in me that it was impossible for me to even think of such a thing?! All I could attribute it to was the need to constantly induce fear and reinforce the boundaries for women as defined by our culture.

I believe finding my partner was the start of my awakening. I refused to get married to someone who would treat me as a lowly woman, there to serve him. I knew there was more for me out there. But how was I going to find him, that one person who would love me the way I am; who would consider me an equal or better yet, consider me more than equal. What's wrong with that? I began to dream big.

Now this wasn't a very easy task since I'm not allowed to date. I went to the meetings that my parents' had arranged where you meet the boy and his family, and you get to talk to him in the other room for about 30 minutes before deciding if you want to spend the rest of your life with him. That's just the way it was and still is for many people. But none of them were it. When I tried to explain this to my family, they would always say, "You can't get everything in a man. You have to be satisfied with less." And I thought to myself: asking for someone to treat you as a human being, as someone of equal value, is not asking for everything. Those who wanted a maid whom they could use for more purposes than one did not deserve me!!

Then I decided to be proactive. Yes - I went on the internet to a marriage site for Indian people. That was an eye-awakening experience! This was a safe and approved way of socializing with the other sex. I learned some pretty interesting things, if you can imagine what the wackos out there are willing to share on the internet! It was also a way for me to speak my truth and be open without any danger or monitoring from anyone. It was the perfect avenue for me to find my soul mate under the restrictions I lived with. And that is exactly what happened.

I met a man who everyone had told me didn't exist. Not only was he on the same path as me and held the same beliefs and values, he also understood my background and had a similar upbringing himself. We understood each other perfectly and we both wanted the same things in life. A lot of things began to change for me when I decided to get married. All of a sudden, my worth increased. Maybe because this was the finale of my journey in this family, I had come this far and was now fulfilling the expected role of my marriage to an Indian boy. And lucky for me, he was the perfect guy for me.

Well, I wouldn't say it was all luck. I realized that I had a power in me to get what I wanted. I actually, for once, stood up for myself. I felt I was worth it, and I made things happen for me. And so I got married and moved in with my husband and his family. Now that would be a whole other story which I will save for another day, if you are interested in knowing. But for now, know that both my husband and I began a search to find ourselves. I knew that I was more than what I was brought up to believe I was; more than what my culture defined me to be.

I was close to thirty now and I may have been book smart but I certainly wasn't street smart. I had to catch up fast, in order to get a decent job. I had to speak. I had to have an opinion. It wasn't useful for me to be in hiding all the time. I had to be social. It was hard but I was determined for myself to become more than what even I thought I was capable of. After all is said and done, I have to take responsibility for myself now. Yes, I was married to a man who had no intention of keeping me like a caged cat. He wanted me to be totally independent. (Uh oh… I was having flashes of how easy it would have been to marry that traditional Indian man; where I would iron his clothes and cook and clean for him while he showered me with… with… with WHAT? More laundry?! No, no - that was no life. That was a false security. Back to reality…)

I had chosen correctly and it was up to me to face my fears of this world which I was brought up to believe was very dangerous. There is no use in blaming anyone, and there was no benefit in being a victim. Only I could save myself. The question was: did I believe I was worth it? And the answer was YES. Even though I had contemplated death many times in my life, now with my new friend in my life, I wanted to create more with him. Despite my fears of the world out there, I pushed myself - *or should I say, was most lovingly pushed by my husband* - to apply for jobs, no matter the location. This time, both of our determination manifested into my attaining a professional job related to my studies. Yeah! I wouldn't be condemned to a life as a bank clerk, after spending close to eight years in university. (No offence to bank clerks here, but it wasn't what I wanted.)

I actually had to move to a new city, and had the opportunity to live all on my own for the first time in my life. It was exhilarating! I had never known such freedom in all my life. Eventually my husband joined me and we settled into a new life together. But this would not be the end of our journey; we both knew that there was something missing. For me, I was at the stage of *is this it?* Am I really following my dreams? Do I love my work? Do I fit in? There was no definitive answer, only more questions and doubts. I was still that quiet girl who was always scared to speak up about what was important to her. Yet I knew I had a great power within me. I was able to manifest some important things in my life: I had found a loving partner, I had found a stable career, things seemed perfect on the surface, but the relationships in which I engaged in especially at work were very limiting and unfulfilling.

I would still holdback my true self. I was a different person at work than at home, and many people may know what this feels like and find this acceptable. But for me, this was not acceptable. I had come so far, and I was unwilling to again play the game of being one person out there and another person inside. I wanted to have the same confidence in my abilities at work as I had sitting at home. I wanted to unleash the creativity and potential that I knew I had stored inside me for a long time. This would imply shedding old beliefs, values and attitudes that didn't serve me any longer. Again, it was both my husband's and my determination to find more that we eventually found the WEL-Systems® Institute.

This would be another major life changing event of my life. My program experiences with WEL-Systems opened a whole new world to me. It showed me how easy it was to change my life, and that the ability to do so lay in no other person than me. I was the expert and always have been. I have lived a life, choosing each moment and receiving a result from what I chose. So how can I ever blame anyone else? If I choose differently, what will happen? Do I dare to even make that choice? I also realized that it wasn't about fitting in with the social systems of work and family and friends. It was about being true to yourself, and if that means being different and not fitting in then so be it. I am in control of only myself and no one else, and if there must be rules in my life those rules will be set by myself only and no one else.

Physically, I had a transformation in my body. Although hard to describe, it is something I have never felt before. I felt the energy that I embody. I felt a connection to myself. I was no longer a robot mechanically living and performing my daily tasks. I had the power to choose and experience much more. I was ALIVE!

I believe I found something in my life that most people spend their entire lives seeking: I have a purpose, a passion and a desire to live a meaningful life. I will not settle for second best, simply because there is no need to. And this does not mean that I don't have obstacles to overcome. They are still there but now I welcome them because each one represents a gift to me. They enable my growth. They give me the ability to always choose, and it makes life interesting!

Going to work everyday has also become an adventure. I no longer feel the need to collude with others or to sacrifice myself in order to fit in. In fact, I realize more and more how unique and different each individual is, and the exploration of this is what I find attractive. The key to working together, for me, is not in the finding of common ground but in the embracing of other's individuality, and recognizing the god within. Because each of us will carry certain behaviours based on our cultural conditioning, I aim to stay away from judging others; and neither do I care to focus on other people's opinion of me. It truly does change the whole perspective on the social systems in which I engage daily.

Specifically, knowing what I know today, I am driven to not only share my awakening with others but I also wish to ignite an awakening in those who are seeking more. I have no regrets about my life, so far. In fact, I am exactly where I want to be at age 30 - and I may not have been on this path if things had been different for me. I am especially passionate about working with women who feel their potential is bound by their culture (whether ethnic or social). I believe every woman, no matter what her background is, has the power within her to create a meaningful life for herself.

As a last thought, I would like to say that no one has the ability to change your life but you. Each of us has the potential and ability to create enormous shifts in our lives if we are willing to step into the unknown. I know this because I did it.

Harjit Shokar was born in London, England, where she spent the early years of her childhood. A certified WEL-Systems® Catalyst and CODE Model Coach™, she also holds a M.A. in Economics. Harjit now lives in Ottawa, Ontario

Dancing Around The Fire

Susan Griffin

      I have always thought of my life as a fairly unremarkable one. I was born in England and I had five parents. That is to say, my grandmother lived with us until her death when I was twelve. My brothers were 13 and 15 years old when I was born. So, I had five adults to take care of me through my early years. I was well cared for, nurtured, indulged… even spoiled!

    I know that I came here with the Fire of my own potential in my belly, and with a deep and sacred quiet inside. I know now that that Fire never left me - it only stayed hidden away until I was ready to reclaim it.

    Stories from my early years speak to the paradox that I carry both the power of voice and the power of silence. My Aunt Betty tells the story of a day out with me and her own two older children. As she waited at the bus stop with me in her arms, her son and daughter standing beside us, I began to sing "Hey Mambo, Mambo Italiano!" apparently in a rather powerful voice. Others at the bus stop stared at my cousins, believing that this huge sound must be coming from one of them and not this tiny thing in my aunt's arms. I continued to sing, with great encouragement from my captive audience, until the bus arrived.

    It is fascinating to me to wonder what happened to that singer so few years later, when in school I became convinced that I was not a good singer at all, and found myself always asked to take my place in the front row in school concerts (being so small) but to please just mime the words (being so tuneless).

Another story tells of the day, around the age of two-and-a-half, that I fired my babysitter. No small feat for someone my size. Apparently, I insisted that I should never be taken to her house again, and that was the end of the matter! It seems I went to this babysitter's home each day for quite some time, until the day I announced that I would not go there again. No apparent evidence of abuse or mistreatment, I simply would not go back there. End of story.

I have no memory of this event, in mind or body, and only know the story as it has been told to me. There must have been something significant in that event for my parents to simply comply with my insistence, and yet I have no sense or fear inside me of having been the victim of some kind of abuse.

My Uncle George gave me the nickname "Gold-dust", for my freckles and as in "silence is golden". He and Aunt Mary, my mother's oldest sister, had five grandchildren close to my age. Mary and George ran a small hotel, with large grounds and an orchard. They also kept a goat (outside) and a parrot and a monkey (indoors). I have vibrant memories of summer Sundays spent there with my cousins. They could be a rowdy lot at times, climbing trees, terrorising the goat, chasing the monkey. I somehow always managed to be the quiet one, never quite in the midst of all the noise and tumult.

These experiences in my early years are not those of a puny and fearful being. They are the experiences of a force to be reckoned with: a Fiery, powerful, self-referenced, fully alive human being. In my adult life, I have often wondered where that person went. Why did she choose to hide and become silent?

How "real" are my early memories? I write here of my own experience of my life, aware that my perceptions, my internal experience of events in my life, may not match the recollections of others who shared those experiences and events. That is the nature of personal experience: it's personal. It's my own experience not someone else's.

I grew up learning to please. I was a good Catholic girl. I went to church, I went to confession, I said my prayers, I did well in school. "Be a good girl. Be quiet, be kind to others, always share, don't be too proud of yourself, don't be too noticeable, don't be pushy, -- and above all don't ask for what you want –wait to be offered or invited, and never, ever question your parents, teachers or clergy. Never challenge authority." These were the rules, and I learned to follow them very carefully. I became quiet, shy, reserved, afraid to speak up or stand out. I grew to be silent and invisible.

I always tried so hard to do and say what was appropriate and acceptable - to never be offensive to anyone - that I learned to censor every thought and action. I learned to examine and analyse every thought before speaking up or taking any action, to the extent that I kept myself silent and immobile for fear of doing or saying something inappropriate.

When I immigrated to Canada, at the age of 18, I had a very pronounced northern England accent. I soon discovered that many people took a great interest in my accent and wanted to hear more, "Oh, listen to that accent, say something else!" Again, I silenced myself in embarrassment. How inappropriate and embarrassing to stand out that way! I worked very hard to suppress that accent and develop a way of speaking that would blend in with those around me.

I spent so much of my life living in compliance with what I came to believe was expected of me, who I learned to believe I was supposed to be, that I completely forgot what it was like to actually BE me. Compliant, programmed, predictable, and oh so easy to get along with! And so often I felt that something was missing, there must be something more. What I have discovered since then of course, is that what was missing was me! Where was Susan Griffin?

I went on to live a very nice, acceptable, appropriate life. I was a good friend, sister and daughter. I worked hard, had the right aspirations, did well in my career… in several careers, in fact.

I married a man who is brilliant, passionate and Fiery. We have created a great life together. Don comes from a very similar background to my own, and so we continued to do all the right and appropriate things together. We lived the lifestyle that was expected of people of our means. We worked hard to own a nice home, travel to wonderful places, raise a brilliant child. We had what we wanted. Life was good!

Yet, I wondered why sometimes there was still that nudging little voice, deep down, hinting that maybe there was something more... What was the matter with me? Would I never be satisfied with what I have?

There really was not much wrong with my life, there just was not enough of me in it! It's clear to me now that much of my life I have searched to find meaning and purpose for myself. For much of my life, I had no truly compelling dreams, no strong opinions of my own, no driving passion for anything in particular. I wore the cloak of who I was supposed to be or expected to be. I immersed myself wholeheartedly and willingly in my roles of wife, mother and consultant - my means of defining myself. Mostly clueless about what I really wanted for myself, my energy was given to fulfilling the intentions of others.

In my early forties, I began to experience bouts of depression. They usually occurred in the winter months and were labelled Seasonal Affective Disorder. By mid-winter, I would usually be feeling a low, dull SADness. Again, I would wonder 'what was the matter with me' and 'what could I possibly have to be depressed about?' I would brush the thought aside - nothing wrong with me that those mid-winter holidays somewhere tropical would not fix.

My father had died from a sudden heart attack in 1989. My mother died in 1992 from cancer. I remember feeling adrift after my mother's death; as though somehow being without parents meant that I was now alone in the world. I felt anchorless. I had my own family; I still had my brothers and their families. I was never really alone and yet I felt so.

There have been a number of significant turning points for me. There are those of us who manage to have one great epiphany and just get it over with -- poof! Big flash of white light and away you go, fully transformed. And there are those like me who enjoy somewhat lesser epiphanies that are nonetheless transformative. Life is never the same, even without the big flash. Much more than "ah-hah!" moments, these are the moments that stop me in my tracks, "gob-smacked" as they would say where I come from. And in that moment, I choose to take another road.

One of the most significant of those moments came for me about eight years ago. It was a moment that set me on the path that would eventually lead me to the WEL-Systems® perspective from which I now live my life.

I remember sitting on the examining table in my doctor's office, on a dull mid-winter day, shivering in one of those silly, barely-cover-your-ass gowns, awaiting the doctor's entry. Not even sure why I was there, other than some vague obligation to do the once-a-year pap test thing. The nurse had already stuck my finger to check my haemoglobin and informed me that I was probably anaemic (I could have told you that) and that I should be taking iron supplements. I listen and I know I won't because iron pills always make me sick.

I sat there staring at the walls… waiting… and noticed that there were two posters: one listed ten signs of perimenopause, the other listed ten signs of major depression. I checked off seven out of ten on each list. No wonder I was miserable! My doctor arrived and performed the requisite prodding and probing, and scribbled a prescription for an iron supplement while I recited my woes relating to her two posters. With much compassion and soothing words, she began to write a prescription for antidepressant medication, and "something to help you sleep"; and of course, I should probably begin hormone replacement therapy as well.

I sat there with tears on my face while this compassionate and dedicated woman, backed by the very best of modern medicine, offered me a potent cocktail that would run my life for me. Clearly, I was not up to the task! In that moment, some part of me awakened, a signal connected, a voice rose from some deep place within and said, "No! I do not want to be drugged! There must be some other way." And it was clear that I would have to find that other way for myself.

The journey that began for me that day - although it began with searching for new ways to achieve overall wellbeing and ease in my life - was to be a journey that would take me into the deepest parts of myself; into the places that had lain dormant, shut down and ignored for so long; into a reawakening of those parts of myself, and into a rekindling of the Fire of my own possibilities.

I began by looking to alternative therapies for depression and menopause: herbal remedies, naturopathic and homeopathic formulas and 'natural' supplements of all kinds. I started to read everything I could find about alternatives to drug therapy, including dietary changes, vitamin supplements, and exercise programs. I researched diligently, through books and the internet and talking to practitioners of various kinds. I eventually devised for myself a daily regimen of vitamins, herbs and supplements designed to address all my needs and various conditions. I did feel much better. I had also quit my stressful job and returned to consulting and contract work, allowing me greater control of when and how I worked. Life was less stressful, somehow easier.

Still something nagged at me, that underlying thought that there must be more to it than this. Another turning point was on the horizon.

Around this time in my life, my dearest friend became ill and eventually died from cancer. My friend had been having ongoing issues with a sore neck and shoulder and had been having regular chiropractic treatment. Eventually even that did not help. Bonnie was in severe and constant pain for about six months before finally being diagnosed with Multiple Myeloma. The disease was aggressive. Tumours were advanced and only partially operable. For two years, I watched my friend endure chronic severe pain, surgery, frequent transfusions, chemotherapy and all its devastating side effects. I tried to support her as much as I could with friendship, companionship and compassion, and in the end there was nothing for me to do but observe the complete breakdown of the physiology of another human being.

I watched the last years of my closest friend's life with great sadness, and with what I have since come to recognise as rage. And I now often wonder, how much rage must my friend have held, shut down inside herself for so long, for her body to turn so completely on itself?

Seeing the amazing number and combinations of drugs that Bonnie had to take on a daily basis, I now noticed the cocktail of vitamins and supplements that I was taking. In my search for 'natural' solutions to my problems, what I had created for myself was simply a different kind of drug therapy than the one my doctor had offered.

The experience of my friend's death really invited me to examine my life and how I lived it, at a much deeper level. I began to think about the notion that what I was still searching for would come not from the outside - in what I could put into my body to achieve health, well being and contentment - but would instead somehow come from inside myself; from what was already present inside me, in my approach to life and how I went about it. I didn't know how to access what I was thinking of, or where to begin, and so my quest continued.

It had also become clear to me that I was looking for something different in terms of the work that I could do. After more than 15 years in the technical writing and communication business, I wanted change. I wanted work that was more meaningful for me and would have value in the lives of others. These two ideas - the search for a life of health and vitality and the search for meaningful work - would soon dovetail and lead me where I needed to go.

I began again to search and research. I read many books and listened to many audiotapes, on all kinds of topics in the realm of personal development and self-discovery. I practiced yoga. I practiced meditation. I tried affirmations. I journaled. I looked for all the ways to discover my life purpose, my true calling, the work I was meant to do. I discovered the world of energy therapies and learned Reiki. I eventually became a Reiki Master and set up a practice offering Reiki to clients. Although I had a number of significant insights and discoveries along the way, and learned much about myself, I knew there was more. There was something deeper and larger to discover. But what was the key? Where was the path that would take me there?

As I looked for ways to use my writing and communication skills to design work that would be the right fit for me, I learned about neurolinguistic programming (NLP). Here was something that would enhance my skills by having a deeper understanding of how we function, and communicate, as human beings. I did some further investigation, found a local NLP Training organization and early in 2001, I signed up for the NLP Practitioner Program. One of the leaders of that program was Louise LeBrun.

As I moved through the seven days of that program, I began to realize that I had found what I came for - and it wasn't NLP! Although NLP laid the groundwork and provided the underpinnings, what truly provided me with the pathway to profound change in my life was the WEL-Systems® models and framework that Louise introduced into that program.

Soon after that NLP program, the WEL-Systems Institute was established. I continued to engage the WEL-Systems programs, through the four levels of Portals Passages certifications, and some of the shorter programs. From that first program experience, my life began to change. I began to reclaim parts of myself that I had not known were lost. I began to discover ways of being that I had forgotten were possible. I had begun the journey home… to myself.

I discovered that I do have dreams and passions of my own; that there are many things that I want for myself in my world; that I have some very strong opinions all my own; that I have plenty to say; that I have deeply held beliefs and values that are mine and are not shaped by the beliefs, values, and attitudes of years of cultural conditioning.

I discovered that I have the capacity to choose for myself how I want my life to unfold, and that in the process of choosing moment-to-moment comes the experience of creating a life that is my own. It is the process of choosing, again and again, that moves me forward. It is my capacity to choose that lets me shape my world and if I do not choose, someone else will choose for me and my world will be shaped differently. And so, it is up to me to do the shaping!

As my journey through the WEL-Systems programs unfolded, Don often wondered who was going to come home each evening, and that clearly speaks to my experience of autopoiesis in action; of creating my life and becoming who I am day-to-day. I am truly blessed to have Don as my spouse and partner on this journey. His continued support and encouragement, his willingness to have his life tilted on a regular basis, his willingness to allow me the space to make my discoveries and go where I needed to go and to go there with me, to the extent of making his own journey into WEL-Systems programs and discoveries of his own.

My discoveries about myself in the Fire of my awakening have been many and vast. I have discovered that I have an immense capacity to sense, to observe, to create and to influence by my actions, by my words, by my presence; that I have great ability for self-expression, to express who I am and what I know in situations and with people that before would have scared me silent; that I can no longer not claim the truth of my own experience - if I hold back, my body soon lets me know about it; that staying in the tough conversations is an ongoing evolutionary process; that when I remain mindfully aware and awake, my curiosity leads me into places and conversations that hold great potential; that new knowledge and growth are available in every connection I make; and that when things do not always unfold the way I want, I am now aware that I have made my choices and that I can choose differently. I can change what I want to change.

My experience of awakening to the Fire within - that Fire energy of creativity, transformation and manifestation - is an ongoing evolutionary process. My journey continues. It has not always been an easy one. I had to step completely outside the realm of what I know that I know, into a place of not knowing; into the restlessness that I had carried inside for so long, and be willing to let go of what I thought I knew and begin to trust the truth of my own experiences. I had to discover my own internal reference points and learn to trust in the brilliance and genius of what moved inside me. I had to be willing to let go of all my masks and cloaks and be seen and heard in the world.

My discoveries about myself have had profound effects on the most important relationships in my life. Those relationships have grown and deepened. As I have begun to engage from a deeper, authentic sense of Self, those relationships are no longer roles in my life - they are growing, organic processes engaged with growing, living, breathing human beings. And my loved ones are up for it!

As I continue to move through my life differently, my personal evolution becomes a mirror where others see the possibilities for their own evolution. Those around me who see the changes and growth in me and the changes in my life, become curious about what I have learned, what I know, how

I got there. In becoming who I am, I have become an invitation to others to seek and to take the first steps in the direction of their own evolution.

In one of the WEL-Systems programs I participated in – one of Gwen McCauley's Creativity for Life experiences – I was working at putting some finishing touches to a painting that I was not quite satisfied with. Gwen watched my efforts for a few minutes before asking about what effect I was trying to create. When I explained my difficulty, Gwen said, "Well Susan, just look at the brush you are using – you might want to think about trying a bigger brush!" I was trying to create sweeping feathery strokes with a small, fine brush. I switched to a large brush and got what I wanted from my painting.

What I learned from that experience was how often in life do we go about things with great intention and purpose, and yet we do not stop to consider the tools we are using to achieve our goals. With the best of intentions and greatest passion, we go about things with tools that are not up to the job. The WEL-Systems approach finally showed me the tools I was looking for and that I already had. I had never before found the tools to look at my life from a different perspective, to look at how I lived my life and the kinds of choices I made, and to look from a different perspective at my own potential and who it was possible for me to become.

Discovering who I am, who I am capable of becoming and what I want in my life, has given me the capacity to create for myself "work" that is meaningful for me and has helped me to design my practice as life coach, workshop facilitator, writer, speaker.

I believe that the purpose of our life in this human existence is to truly live this life; to live fully alive, aware and awake to our own potential. To live every bit of our life, all of the joy and desire, sorrow or despair, love and exhilaration, fear or desperation – it's all life and it is ours to claim and live with passion and intention.

A number of my friends and clients have spoken with me recently about the notion of Sacred Contracts. They speak to the idea that we each come here with a specific purpose and specific contracts with other individuals, and that to fulfill our purpose or destiny we must live our life to fulfil those contracts. The notion of a predetermined destiny does not feel right for me. I believe that our true destiny is to choose, moment-to-moment-to-moment, to move forward in our life, to become who we are, our ever-unfolding Self.

If I have a contract at all in this life, it is a contract with my Self to become who it is possible for me to become - authentically true to myself, fully alive and awake.

I'm rather fond of a quote, from Mavis Leyrer aged 83, *"Life's journey is not to arrive at the grave safely, in a well preserved body, but rather to skid in sideways, totally worn out, shouting "Holy shit, what a ride!"* I hope that I will make my exit as gracefully as Mavis!

Use a really big brush and paint your life with great sweeping strokes!

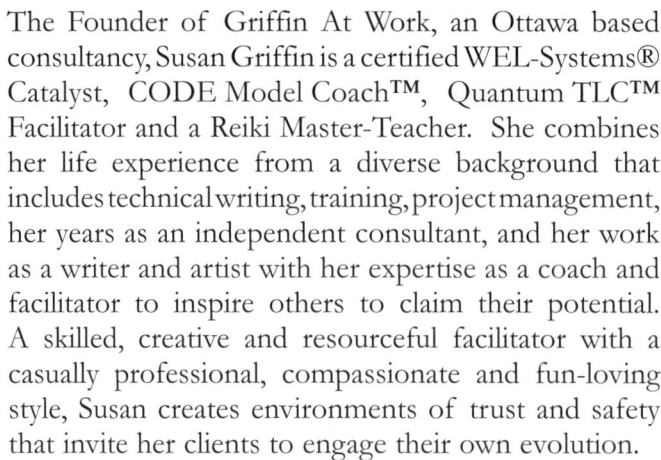

The Founder of Griffin At Work, an Ottawa based consultancy, Susan Griffin is a certified WEL-Systems® Catalyst, CODE Model Coach™, Quantum TLC™ Facilitator and a Reiki Master-Teacher. She combines her life experience from a diverse background that includes technical writing, training, project management, her years as an independent consultant, and her work as a writer and artist with her expertise as a coach and facilitator to inspire others to claim their potential. A skilled, creative and resourceful facilitator with a casually professional, compassionate and fun-loving style, Susan creates environments of trust and safety that invite her clients to engage their own evolution.

Dancing Around The Fire

The Passage Back to Me

Koreen Kimakowich

Introduction

Imagine spending your lifetime seeking... searching... longing for that place where you belonged, not because someone said you belonged but because you simply knew you did. We all belong. Instinctively, I knew that and my 'knowing' was soon to be fulfilled.

I knew there was a space out there, somewhere in this vast land called Earth that I could claim as mine to stand in; just waiting for me to discover and step into. With a willingness to take the journey that would lead me through miles of emotion, information and energy, I discovered much about that space. The most significant discovery would be the re-acquaintance I would make with me: who I was, am and would become. I learned that space wasn't waiting for me to step into but rather, as I chose me, I became the space; and the space became filled with me. My journey has been my lifetime and my lifetime, my journey.

For those many years that I questioned my belonging-ness, I am now aware that I needed to be curious and enquiring – which is where and who I am today – rather than uncertain and afraid. *Where* I am is physically, spiritually, energetically with me. *Who* I am is my authentic self - and it is painful to be anyone other than that. I am comfortably living the full expression of my self, shaping my world and in doing so, letting you know of your brilliance, starting with your innate and ever-available ability to shape your own world as you so desire.

What did it take for me? Simply put: a breath. Taking a breath in a moment where I would have otherwise been holding it. One simple, purposeful breath opened me up to the possibilities of me; creating the space for the possibilities to have passage and movement; and for the constant flow to facilitate the purpose of the energetic messaging, the learning, the evolving. All this happening in my body. That took choosing to trust that breath is not just about ensuring life but rather, it is the life force of and within me, within each of us. The restless wanting and waiting was, in fact, me. I was all and everything it would take to find *The Passage Back to Me*.

The cultural conditioning I would experience in my lifetime - in the world of deeply entrenched beliefs, values and attitudes borne of parent/child relationships, religiosity, school, work, teachings of good/bad, right/wrong - compels me to share this story. I should not have escaped the wrath of it all, and yet the all-knowing of me was relentless in having me notice that I mattered. This is not about blame or fault, or anyone doing or being a series of things to me; rather, it is about having been born all-knowing and then, as a matter and practice of cultural conditioning, I became undone. Innocently, as the generations before me, and undone just the same. This conditioning was as much a cycle of habits as my own individual ones would become. I was a fractal of the grander scheme of things.

God & Learned Responses: Lessons Learned

From the point of my first lesson learned - no doubt as an infant, perhaps even in the womb - up until my turning point at thirty nine years of age, my life would have all the trappings of a life confined. Fear would be my primary jailor. Fear of my parent's death, specifically my mother. Fear of god. Fear of what being bad meant: what was bad and how would I know? Fear of being wrong. Fear of my own death. Fear of me. And the most significant of them all, fear of living a fearful life. From these fears would come many vices to counteract the constriction - attempts to gain control of my life, my self; to make it a less dangerous place and have my life be mine again. All were intelligent responses in their day and all were devoid of any evolutionary properties.

Those vices would have names and there were many that I would invite into my life as a way of living. Obsessive compulsive. Depression. Eating disorders. All of them, though given names in the allopathic model of the world, I now know were manifested as a way of getting my attention. It wasn't about the depression but rather, it was about what lay beneath the depression: that disconnecting from myself seemed more inviting than living fully. Depression was much less painful than the alternative.

I had manifested the distractions so I did not have to notice my self. Clearly, this was no way to live and yet it was the only way I knew how to live – certainly, at least, at an intellectual level. Thankfully, the full and authentic expression of me never completely relinquished its presence within me. In fact, as I ponder it, the much deeper aspects of me were always willing to flirt with the world my intellect saw as dangerous. I am thankful for that. I am thankful that I heard the constant call of my "self".

The first time (in the throes of culturally conditioned response) that I would detect 'me' - my call, my voice, my sound, my truth - was around the event/ritual of saying the rosary with my mom, and my brother and sister. Typically, we would be doing this if we were in need of something. Kneel down and ask god, and if he chooses, so it shall be. My mother rounded us up ("the three little ones", as we were always referred to) to recite the rosary. I knew somewhere deep within me that this couldn't be my life, needing to constantly beg outside of me for peace within me. There was nothing peaceful or reassuring about having to do that. I recall now, as a seven-year-old, the internal conversations; the questioning of it - my voice, my sound, my truth showing up where, as a rule, only cultural conditioning had permission to be.

I can't be sure of the percentage of readers who have experienced having to say the rosary, but as a kid just wanting to get outside to "play, play, play"; I can tell you this was definitely a long, drawn-out and boring experience. An inchanting affair. At seven years old, what could I possibly have to atone for anyway? The underlying message of why we were doing this, and subsequently the imprint that experience left on me, was that my fate - my life - was in someone else's hands, always.

Life was to be lived in a state of perpetual atonement, always having to forfeit pleasure for penance. Deep inside however, I knew instinctively that that wasn't the case. But as a seven-year-old, how do you articulate that to mommy? You don't - and so you conform. Disingenuous as I was in reciting the prayers, I said them anyway - hostage to the cultural conditioning of my childhood, fearful that god would detect the falsity and I would be punished severely by a god I instinctively knew didn't exist. I expected to be punished, and so I chose accordingly. Expectations tend to be realized.

Interestingly, when things were going badly in my house, it usually revolved around my father being in what we could call a 'bad mood'. I now know that mood had far more impact than any 'mood' should have. We endured at the hands of the remnants of his haunting past; unhealed and open wounds of his conditioning, now playing out in his children's lives; a conditioning that even his own beautiful, loving and adoring mother could not protect him from. All he could do now was strive to control and keep the monsters at bay. While he was bigger and stronger, he was still wounded. In his darkest hours, his mind perceived us to have become those monsters. At least, that is my story of it. I am, after all, my father's daughter. This was the cycle of his life, and so it was the cycle of ours. It made me love him no less; and I am fortunate that in my lifetime, there was the space that I chose to step into and discovered that the cycle could indeed be broken.

When things would go awry, my mother would gather us up after dinner for a succession of days. We'd toddle off into the living room; take our places 'on our knees', leaning up against the unusually long couch, and recite the rosary aloud with her. A chant, if you will, and I know she was doing and being all that she knew how to be to make it a better place for us to live in. As my memory and experience recall it, each time out I would ask god to make my father be in a better mood, be nicer to me and come back upstairs to be with us again. He was never far physically, but where 'he' went otherwise, I can only surmise to this day.

Familiar as the cycle was to my biological family, I never became used to the fact that a father could be this way. I cannot find blame in him, rather, I am filled with pain at what the terror of his childhood must have been that he would live his days this way with us. Though the tendency might be to focus on the issue of the mood, this story is not about that at all. It is much more about how I was taught young that if you wanted your life to change and be better, you had to be a really good little girl. This meant that you had to believe in god and then ask permission from someone you had never met before, never seen, had no proof even existed other than by the stories of others who, themselves, had never met or seen this entity before, either. What I knew innately inside was that I didn't believe in god - and would the god I didn't believe in send me to hell for that. Conflicted? Absolutely, and I wasn't alone.

The catalyst for forming this belief that god (that entity residing outside of me) was the only chance I had for my life to be better, was solidified by the fact that each time we would engage in the ritual of saying the rosary, my father indeed would find himself in a better mood; and that we would once again have permission to engage with him. It would become safe again. What more proof did I need that god answers prayers?

I was not aware, at that time, of the habituated cyclical nature of us humans. What is evident to me today is that this wasn't about prayers being answered at all. It was instead about each of us running our habituated responses to our circumstances, and the cycle running its course. Part of that cycle was his 'good mood'.

Our life responses are driven by how we perceive our world. Is it a safe or a dangerous place? What we conclude becomes for us central nervous system, wired-in responses. Case in point: as an adult, I am now able to look back and recognize that we were indeed all running our survival strategies, in great anticipation of that part of the cycle we call the 'honeymoon' stage; and we were all attempting to survive something different. What could be the intelligence for any of us to run such strategies? Today, I can only tell you what my intelligence might have been - at least, at an intellectual level. As bad as his bad moods were, when he was on the opposite end of that continuum, his good moods brought jubilation times a hundred. In some ways then, the only way to experience the exhilarating feeling of jubilation was to create the stage for it. Not sure which came first, the chicken or the egg; and as the cycle ran itself, it no longer mattered. An intelligent response to our unraveling lives; a way of life, a way of living.

What in that moment I concluded were prayers – mine, being answered by god - today I recognize as a collective family strategy running itself. Learned responses to our dangerous environment combined with our innate desire to survive it, no matter how much it felt like hell on earth.

As a child, sponge-like in absorbing it all, these presented as ongoing miracles of prayer. Even in my amazement and wonder at these constant experiences of miracles perpetuated by god, a much deeper enquiry stirred inside me. How could it be that the god I was taught to love unconditionally and fear endlessly could make things so good, and yet could also be so cruel as to make them so bad? Cruel god, cruel father. Could I survive this?

Surviving BVAs

I could and I did survive, by trusting that I was enough to see me through all the way back to my self. In that moment of trust, I was rendered a well-lit, long, wide and infinite passageway. It became well lit only when I chose to set my foot on its course. My Light was leading the way.

As my Light radiated all that was my now and beyond, what came into focus was a plethora of beliefs, values and attitudes (BVA's) that had been thrust upon me and had become the driver of my responses to my life. These were the result of programming of the meekest, most vulnerable and most impressionable – of the child that I was. The Light also illuminated the realization that I could revisit each one of the BVAs as I chose, and collapse them as it made sense to 'me' to do so. There were many in and out of my awareness that would collapse. The revisiting couldn't and didn't take place in my intellect because that is not where the habituated responses originated. Rather, my intellect was the conduit for their demonstration outside of me. It is from our intellect that all of us reveal or give snippets of what is going on inside of us. Cloaked as we are, we are always nonetheless revealing snippets of us. It presents itself in a combination of energetic fields, body cues and verbal language.

In trusting me/my Light, I came to learn that these shifts - these new considerations - in order to have any hold would have to be introduced at a much deeper level, where in fact the old strategies had taken root; at a cellular level, in my cellular memory; my molecular bits of emotion; that place where all of our deeply embedded responses lay and limit the degree to which we have access to our brilliance. I would have to be willing and able to go to that place I'd held as dark; that place from which I had, so far, been protected by living only from the neck up. My journey would have to take a downward and inward turn; back to the source of all of the secrets to which I'd held myself captive; where the pain barricaded me from the onslaught of unthinkable displeasure. "Yes! Go there, Koreen! Go right there. Go within. Go now!" I heard me, and I listened.

Being brave and courageous, once there, I discovered my brilliance in all of its colors of celebration, patiently awaiting my arrival. Through that rekindled relationship with my brilliance, all I had to do was trust myself fully and I would learn that I was, am and always will be much more than I was taught to believe I was. One cannot deny the vibration of their own spirit; their signal from self. Trusting long enough allowed me to see, feel, hear, smell and delight in my own brilliance, through the vibration that while not dormant, had laid all too silent for too long. The vibration was the metabolizing of thirty-nine years of accumulated energetic information suppressed and denied permission to process. Tears never cried for fear I'd pay a bigger price than I already had. "Stop crying or I'll give you something to cry about". I never chanced coming to know what the darkness of that 'something' was. Thoughts never given voice/sound for fear they would be ridiculed, minimized, used against me. To trust that I would be heard only had to be broken once for me to know to stay silent. I would learn that early and well, and would be silent. All this in the name of survival. Up to that point, I had clearly experienced my world as a dangerous place; one where survival was tantamount, with a little living on the side.

Possibility of Purpose

As I write this passage, I am mindful of the first time that I became aware of the journey of my life and the possibility of purpose. My purpose was for me to choose.

Close to ten years ago, if not more, I attended the final appointment with a psychiatrist I'd been seeing for an eating disorder. At that time, I was about thirteen years into allowing this vile disease time in my life; time to own me. I had been going to these appointments for just over a year. I would meet faithfully with her once a week and would relay and repeat all of the pitiful, self-absorbing, victim-laden sad stories of my life, holding all of them and the people in them responsible for 'giving' me this dreadful disease.

I'd been grudgingly introducing antidepressants into my body, knowing fully that they had not and would not make this disease go away. In retrospect, unquestionably the anorexic/bulimic behavior was merely the demonstration of trying to take back control in what seemed like an out-of-control life; to gain control, or the appearances of control, anywhere I could.

The initial intelligence behind engaging in the behavior was that thirteen years previous, my partner of four years chose to leave the relationship. Of the many stories I had told myself about why she chose that, the one that took hold was the one about how I had become unattractive; had gained some weight and if I just lost a few pounds, she'd come back to me. I struggled to regain control of this situation, at all costs. Sound like a familiar story?

Fast forward thirteen years. I had now been in a stable, loving and fulfilling relationship for ten years, though we were never to discuss my 'disease'. On that enlightened day, I sat in that tiny office - a physical environment struggling to exude a calm and soothing mood. I recognized myself to be in exactly the same intellectually and emotionally disheveled state that I had arrived in a year earlier, when we first commenced for our fifty-minute hour of conversation. Nothing had changed but everyone else around me was feeling better for my going.

Regrettably, I was more active in the behaviors than ever and experiencing no end in sight (indicative of a wired-in response, if there ever was one). The weekly meetings simply became interwoven into the habits of my days. What was most telling about that last appointment, however, was that this very well educated and learned individual broke the bad news to me that living with the eating disorder may be something I would have to resign myself to doing for the rest of my life.

Eureka! In that moment, I was jolted awake to myself. Whatever the intelligence was in engaging in this behavior that had become a clung-to habit - and more!... a way of life for me for seventeen years total - it became clear to me that I had chosen to engage them and it would take me, and only me, choosing something different now. I had chosen to engage and I would need to be the one to choose to disengage.

With the original intelligence of it long absent, I recognized this dis-ease as nothing more than a programmed response to my life. This insight weakened the hold the dis-ease had had on me all of those years. It was no longer as big and insurmountable as it had seemed a moment prior. The message of hopelessness given sound through the Doctor's allopathic voice, caused the wave of my own resourcefulness to erupt in my body with Fire, the element of transformation, spewing everywhere. The Flame of me burst into life, never to be embers again.

It indeed, would not be she who cured me. This dis-ease was my responsibility, and curing and healing were also my responsibility. The ability to heal myself was available to me. Down and in was where the intelligent response of that day, fourteen years previous, was masterminded and that is where I would have to go to reconfigure; to collapse the limiting beliefs of the day and become resourceful for my self. It was for me, in all of my innate brilliance, to claim this and own it so that it would no longer own me.

It was clearly time to get out of my own way. It was time for the culturally conditioned me to take a break and allow the identity of me - who I knew myself to be deep within - to have voice, sound, authentic internally-referenced choice. This was not an intellectual realization, rather an energetic one. That hit came from deep within my body, and it was evident that I would have to go there if I wanted the 'more' that awaited me.

Knowing what I know now, it was no accident that in my life - given the conditioning that I experienced - my response to what I held as a 'sorry' life would play out in the area of my solar plexus where Fire, the element of transformation, resides.

This is the area in our bodies that speaks to the degree to which we hold ourselves powerful or powerless in our lives. In that 'eureka' moment, I was able to get a peek at the 'who else' of me that lived there and was available to me, and that she/me/I was, undeniably, enough! How liberating it was in that moment of trust and discovery.

The Bond of an Unshakeable Trust

This is a story of personal triumph. In an unsuspecting and unexpected moment of reconnecting with myself, I noticed it and knew instantly I was and am all I need. I am enough. I had no need or reason to fear myself and the stories and experiences of my life. I had been creating all of it, with an innate knowing that it would bring me back to me. The difference was that I was now aware of choice and change, and that both were available and achievable at quantum speeds. What the external world couldn't cure in over seventeen years, I was able to heal my self of in thirty minutes by seeking and trusting my internal self. Today, I embrace the bond of an unshakeable trust with my self.

This Is...

This is a depiction of the degree to which cultural conditioning, devoid of respect for the individual genius of us all, can be vicious in its being imposed. I am sad for my father and today, knowing what I know, have mindfully chosen to be kinder to him in these final stages of his life than what he would experience in his early years. He knows that I love him unconditionally, and so too my mother for what she held as our chance for survival.

This is not a representation of anger towards or debating the existence of god. I am acutely aware that I could not have found 'here' if I had not created in this life, on this pass, every moment of the 'there' from which I have come. The 'there' included a god that I believed in for fear of the wrath that I would suffer if

I didn't believe in him. Today, I am clear that god in the context of a supreme, all-knowing godforce doesn't exist outside of me, rather god in the context of supreme, all-knowing godforce is me. I am it. Having freed my self of the despairing cycle of the teachings of the existence of god, the cultural conditioning imposed upon me as a child has simply fallen away.

In a moment of becoming brave and courageous in the face of my own search for peace, I chose to breathe; and bring my attention - the signal of me - beyond my intellect and down into my body to the base of my spine. The gate to the resourceful vibration of me opened and I simply settled into it; settled into me, and I would never be that culturally conditioned self again.

Every cell in my body experienced the quake of the matter of me. It was a most welcoming and recognizable internal vibration. The cellular interactions were mine and mine alone, with the conditioned ones collapsing and the new ones accepting the invitation to be, through energetic processes. I awoke to my self. I became fully conscious, and I could not un-know or deny what I had just experienced.

Some would say the greatest revelation was to discover that my Self knew there was no longer an intelligence in embracing the eating disorder amongst the many of the un-resourceful aspects of what I held as my identity. It was simply that my intellect didn't know how to interrupt the pattern; didn't know how to stifle the strategy. Once I stopped trying to figure it out, my body processed for me what my mind, even in seventeen years, couldn't. While that insight was welcomed and true for me, the greatest revelation of that day was that I was indeed, unmistakably all I needed.

It is worth stating again here: the all-knowing, all-supreme godforce that I was taught to both love and fear, did not exist outside of me at all. In fact, I was and am it. When I discovered I was it, I realized: if "I Am the Source", I need only love and not fear. I have experienced and seen the very essence of me, my Light. In that moment of experiencing the energy of me,

I did not ask in language for any of the un-resourceful states to leave me, rather I trusted and knew that my body - open and available to me - would know exactly what it needed to do. While our intellect, with all of its perceptual filters, can convince us of just about anything, our body does not have the ability to lie. It was to trust it to do/be exactly what it needed to do/be without imposing my intellect. For a disorder that consumed close to half of my life, on that day I would leave the room having claimed it and, as a result, free of it – never, ever, looking back!

It took choosing to trust that I was more than the matter-based, fallible, sinful being I was told that I was. I have likened the trusting to this metaphor: in the world of the trapeze artist, typically the artist can see the next trapeze awaiting their grasp. The trust I speak of however, is about not being able to see the awaiting trapeze until you choose to release the one that is about to snap and plunge you into your culturally conditioned purgatory. Letting go and trusting that the trapeze will be there, and then feeling it take hold of your grasp.

Rights of Passage: The Passage Back To Me

As a right of passage and as a young, impressionable, god-fearing little girl, I learned early that I was always to take my cue from outside of me, no matter how much it hurt and didn't make sense. I bring that forward here, because it is that the power of cultural conditioning can never be underestimated. Why? Because it embeds itself at a cellular level. Out of our awareness, we become the program of our cellular memories until we come to discover that programmed as we are, we actually get to create our experiences and choose differently if we aren't enjoying the results of our most recent choice. Moment to moment choice!

I became responsible for my self. All of me! I was no longer looking for space in which to stand and take my place. The very place I stood in opened up and there I was, surrounded and supported by all of my energetic me; by all of my brilliance. In one fell swoop, I had it all back and I was instantly recognizable to my self. With that, a new choice point to propel me into my perpetual, ever evolving self.

And so, the passage back to me began. A breathtaking series of revealing experiences: that was and has become my right of passage; my right to evolve.

Blips on the Radar Screen

My darkest moments were those that led me to the brightest Light; to that place where I discovered how to repeatedly shape my world rather than be shaped by it. It was truly my past finding me in the 'now' and knowing. I have shared with you here, an excerpt of healing as taken from my book, "The Passage Back to Me". The passage back from a day of desperation of enormous proportions that would always keep me at arms length from my self. More importantly though, this is a story of pure will/ability/desire, propelled by an innate knowing that fear of living couldn't possibly be all that there was.

The diseases and disorders I so intelligently embraced as my identity, started out not unlike tiny, energetic and very important blips on the radar screen of my very energy affluent existence….my body. My response in cultural conditioning's finest hour, and we all have our stories of how we became that. It is to notice what you know innately to be your blips on the screen looking to get your attention, and then get curious about what they are getting your attention about.

No matter the manifestation, no matter the issues that present in your life, that have caused your own searching, this passage back, to starting your future, is as much available to you as it had always been to me. It becomes then, choice, and whether or not you choose to choose differently, for the first time.

A telling of me was always going to manifest as I found my own healing. I must speak of it, to it, and about it, that you will know, and then, have choice, not around what I'd held as my

<u>dis</u>-ease, rather around your <u>dis</u>-ease, whatever it looks, feels like. Is the blip on your screen big enough that you can name it?

Though it was close to ten years ago now in the psychiatrist's office that I would be given a second of a glimpse of me, it would be some four years after that that I would discover where that glimpse would take me. What I know now is that it didn't have to take four more years.

My World is Safe

In 2003, my path would find me in a space that was safe, and willing to have me exercise my will, ability and desire to reconnect with my self. I claimed it all, and own it all. In doing so, it could no longer own me. I call it a healing, and it is much more expansive than that. It was a coming home. To know what living really looks, feels, tastes, smells, and sounds like!! Not only did I become responsible for all of it all from that moment on, but now awakened, I realize I was and am indeed responsible for all of those years previous to my awakening as well. There is no better place from which to stand in one's life than being personally responsible for your life, at cause. If I am not standing there, then I am at effect, and that is likened to being the victim, in, and of my life. Standing at cause, when we choose that, one's life becomes blameless, victimless, and an extremely enlightened one! In choosing that, unexpectedly my world became a safe place.

Prior to these experiences, I had been taught that something could only be believed when they saw it. Matter based, living tangible proof of an existence or occurrence. As I welcomed the space for new considerations, living at cause, I came to experience the significance of knowing that when I believed it, I would see it. My dear readers, that one concept alone can open the flood-gates to your own expansion. Take a breath, and entertain just that, and that when you believe it you will see it, and notice the internal calm enveloping you.

Trust that the letting go is the claiming, and that when you do that, the learning comes, and it becomes time to move forward in your life with the new learning.

Excerpts of Healing – Conclusion

These writings, excerpts of my healing, are a snippet of my journey, simply stated. A story of my past that without it, I would not be in my now, and knowing. The intent was to share with you that point of me that noticed and knew it was time to reconnect with me, find me, find my voice, be my voice and live finally authentically. With that, I invite you to notice what you have chosen not to notice of your own living, and what strategies you engage in to ensure not noticing your self, in your life. Then, consider new responses that are not determined in the intellect, but rather spoken loudly and clearly to you from your body. What would happen if you stopped all of it, all of the noises that aren't you? What would you notice? Don't be afraid, what you just heard was you, calling to you! Go there!

As you've allowed this story to pass by your eyes, travel into the filters of your own intellect and do let the words rest and resonate ultimately in your body, and then most importantly pay attention to, check in with, how and what reactions your body is having to the story. That is the true telling of you, and with each check in, with each moment you choose to pay attention, get curious about how it is what I have to say, is affecting you the way that it is, in your BODY! It is the first point of taking and being responsible and living at cause. Those feelings you are having are all about you!

Koreen Kimakowich, Founder of Awakening Wave, is a WEL-Systems Catalyst and CODE Model Coach™. With over 18 years in Law Enforcement, Koreen has brought wellness discussions into the profession, in both one-on-one conversations and in large group conference settings. Koreen brings safety and wisdom into her conversations with those who seek to live their lives more fully. She has developed concentrated applications for actual prevention of harassment and discrimination in the workplace drawing on the WEL-Systems® concepts. She welcomes the opportunity to journey with you as you discover your own personal resourcefulness as it lies within you.

Walking the Labyrinth

Anita Allen

In the following pages, I would like to share with you some of the discoveries that I have made with the help and insights available through a WEL-Systems® perspective. Elegant in its simplicity and profound in its implications for living, this perspective has offered me a platform for seeing my life differently. It has empowered me to craft a life that is a unique and authentic expression of who I am. In the process of creating a life filled with meaning and passion, I have discovered an incredible capacity for change and a renewed zest for playing the game of life full-tilt! My newly acquired comfort in uncertainty is much like a walk through a labyrinth where each mindful step offers a sense of mystery, adventure and sacredness. I am honored to share this journey with you for the next few minutes and pages.

Here I sit in the wee hours, having risen with the moon. The sight of a blank computer screen is daunting at this hour. I woke a few minutes ago with tumbling thoughts coursing through my body causing my legs to twitch and tell me they cannot remain still any longer. As I hobbled across the darkened bedroom clutching my notebook, I stifled an ironic laugh at the whole notion of being hobbled and moving furtively when my muse comes calling at this hour. My muse is no shrinking violet, and tonight she reveals herself in the metaphor of Sekhmet, the Egyptian goddess whose name means, "She Who is Powerful".

I wonder why it is that she beckons... no, demands my attention!... as the household sleeps. The soft, dark under belly of the day is where I stalk the thoughts that circle as fragments of something larger. These half formed creatures will only reveal themselves and create a web of connection once captured and placed on the page. I feel a sense of urgency as they flit through my awareness. I don't want them to pass me by. By the light of day they look different and I tend to dismiss them. At night they drag me from my bed. They seduce, they beckon and they demand.

At this late hour as my thoughts circle around the Egyptian goddess, Sekhmet, I am pondering her mythical bloodlust, her dual nature as destroyer and healer/creator. Sekhmet embodies the full continuum of the feminine. She is soft, receptive and nurturing. She has also been given attributes such as 'destructive', 'fiery', and in motion as she rampages. It is her energy that dismantles the old so that new forms can emerge once again from the fertile void. As a metaphor for feminine wholeness, she demonstrates that we are large enough to contain all the aspects of this fire energy, irrespective of our gender.

Fire is an interesting energy. It warms and comforts us. It helps nourish us. It can also be destructive, devouring everything in its path making room for new forms to emerge in its charred wake. We live side by side with fire in our lives and we are taught to respect it. Fire, in the language of The CODE Model™ represents a wide range of words that often come loaded with meanings; words such as pain, fear, rage, creativity, passion or vitality. The word "fire" can represent this entire continuum without emotional attachments. It also implies movement since a fire is always in motion as the flames dart and flicker. Fire has played a supporting role in our evolution as we have learned to harness its energy.

Fire is an essential element in the natural world and its energy is present in each of us as an expression of our vital force. In our culture we are ambiguous about our fire. On one hand, we don't wish to appear overly passionate and excitable, neither do we want to reveal the full measure of our fear, pain or rage to a world perceived to sit in judgment of anything outside a prescribed range of "normal" behavior. To judge fire as anything other than a natural expression of energy flies in the face of nature itself. Fire as an element or energy is neither good nor bad. It simply is. It, like Sekhmet, is a continuum.

As I sit at the keyboard my awareness of how much I have to say and the many places where I am silent is pressing up against me. There is a growing restless within that is mirrored by the rustling of the leaves outside my window. A gentle yet persistent movement that is paradoxically easy to live with and difficult to ignore. Tonight there is softness in the dark and the edges feel far away as I revel in the crucible of my sleeping family. The moonlight softens the darkness with its cool light, another expression of fire, and illuminates the corners in my mind and heart that I have been reluctant to look into fully. The embers of transformation lie waiting to be fanned into life. Tonight, as thoughts of Sekhmet rise with the moon, my restlessness, my own fire, finds expression through the purring of fingers on a keyboard.

Why have I remained quietly nestled within my own thoughts for so long? Where is my voice? I realize that I hold a belief that is common to so many, that I have nothing original to say. Underneath that belief lays another, I will be judged mercilessly for what I choose to say. The barbs of shame lie just below the surface. "Who do you think you are?" "What do you know?" If that is the case, how could I have anything worth sharing as a writer?

I wonder what I have to write about that will be interesting or unique. I wonder if I have anything to say that will make a difference your life – in mine? And then I realize that that voice is not my own. Although it has been with me since I can remember. Always mocking, deflating, hurling insults and belittling, it is not my voice at all. It belongs to no one in particular and everyone in general. That voice may have at times kept me safe in my younger years. It allowed me to fit in where I needed. It made me acceptable as a peer, respectful of the adults in my life, predictable, manageable and generally, in later years has counseled me to coast along in unchallenged mediocrity.

This voice has given me an excuse to not participate fully in my life at times. I have worn its mask and substituted its truth for my own. Its message falsely reassures me that I should simply blend into the scenery. I'm nothing special, no one to take note of. "Lock down!" it commands. "Nice girls don't get angry or share opinions they haven't been asked for. Don't rock the boat. Go with the flow. You might hurt someone. It's too late to choose something else. You have to finish everything that you start" are just a few of its favorite mantras.

That is the 'voice of reason'. It has kept me moving in one track for a very long time. It had forged an identity for me that had grown too small and tight to be ignored. After reading a story about how elephants are trained to work on plantations I made the realization that often in my life I've behaved like one of those elephants. To train a young elephant, it is tied to a big log and it learns that every time it wanders too far the chain around its ankle tightens, preventing further exploration. By the time it is a mighty, fully grown elephant, all that it takes to keep it in place is a little stick. It never questions the reality of its situation or perceives how it has changed as it grew into a powerful force.

One of my sticks has been a profession that I used to define myself. I built an entire identity around it, beginning at the tender age of sixteen. I choose Physiotherapy as a goal and I worked very hard to make it a reality. After years of practicing its art and science, I have come to realize that I cannot define myself based on it any longer. I am much more than one role. As I have become more aware of my authentic self, I have realized that I don't need to restrain myself. I have challenged the validity of the 'voice of reason' and reclaimed my own true note only to discover that I can leave the stick behind and move along differently in the world.

It has taken a great deal of courage to choose to move beyond an identity that I have invested so much time, effort and money in. My husband has lived with the specter of my role as business owner and therapist for most of our marriage. It had become an integral part of who I was. The fact that Physiotherapy and clinic ownership were goals that I spent half of my life bringing into reality and that I am skilled at playing these roles made it even more seductive to follow the siren song of what was expected and accepted. All the while, I had been running from the fire that would transform my life and set me free to choose a life that is a fuller representation of who I am.

As things began to unravel in my business and personal life, I realized that I needed to make different choices. On the outside, I looked very much in control. I was expanding my clinics and I had a great team in place to support it. I was a new Mom. All my dreams were coming true. Everything I had worked for was materializing. Instead of feeling elated, I felt like I had lost myself. Indeed I had. The illusion had become so thick and I had moved so far away from the voice of my authentic self that it was barely a whisper.

I remember having an incredibly vivid dream in which I was running frantically from place to place with fatal snakebites, knowing that death was imminent. That dream rocked me to my core. In retrospect, it was a very prophetic metaphor for the transformation that was about to occur in my life. It did signal a death, but it was the death of an illusion. With nothing more than the vague glimmer of a survival instinct that was awoken in my dream, I embarked on the process of excavating my authentic self. Those processes lead me to the place where I now stand. I have connected deeply to what is true and meaningful in my life and my journey as a fledgling writer has begun.

For as long as I can remember I have loved language - the way that words arrange themselves together on a page like brush strokes in a painting. The image contained in each stroke unfolds into a mesmerizing whole and as the reader I can construct my own vision within myself. Yes, I love the beauty of words.

My first inclinations were to be a writer. My young artist suffered many blows in learning to discern fact from fiction. As imaginary worlds co-mingled with daily life, I learned quickly that making things up could be considered lying – a punishable offence. It could also lead to relentless mocking from classmates. For example, I wondered then - and I still do now, how do we all know what colour the sky is? Does it look different to each of us? Do you see something different than I do? I can now, with experience and more eloquence add - we may have enough language to create a common description, but how do we know that those descriptors represent the same experience for both of us? Back then, there was only one 'true' way to view the world and I learned that I had better get on board with that. I decided it was much safer to read stories than to write them.

The rustling of leaves outside my window continues and my thoughts are turned to the myriad of ways in which I continue to feed my passion for language. My collection of books was the beginning. They are like old friends and often hard to part with even when it becomes necessary to make room for new ones. They have been my gateway to so many places. They mark the phases of my life like the growth rings in a tree. I have passed through many stages from Dr. Seuss through Nancy Drew stories, adventure, romance, cooking, personal evolution, and now more and more books about writing.

Growing ever more restless, I look around my life and have discovered not only have I surrounded myself with books about writing, I have filled my life with writers. Some have published, some are on their way and others hold it as a personal spiritual practice. For all of them it is a medium of self-discovery. The pages they create are snap shots of their evolution. I hold each of their voices as unique. Each offers a new perspective to consider.

Along the way I have asked myself, "Who would I become if I joined their ranks? Who would I become if I freed myself from my web of limitation? What becomes possible in my life, my home, and my family and for anyone else that I touch when I become courageous enough to move beyond this place?" I reached the conclusion that it would require me to be willing to discover my own unique voice and to become shameless about what I had to say. It would require that I release any external reference points and trust my own truth.

As I shed my veils and stand fully exposed and completely unencumbered, how far and how fast can I fly? I am unwilling to leave this world without knowing. The twist is that unless I begin this journey, I will find myself leaving this world sooner rather than later. Even as I write this, the 'voice of reason' is judging it to be overly dramatic in spite of the fact that it bubbles up unsolicited from someplace deep inside me. I DO know that I can no longer deny what I know about myself and that the immensity of this Fire, if not in flow, will find another way to express itself in my body. I have a choice and moving toward further discovery is far more compelling than running away from the perceived consequences touted by the dimming 'voice of reason'.

As I released the beliefs that pinned me in place like a butterfly under glass, I have had to become honest with myself about the strategies that I had employed to keep myself under wraps. The number of times that I chose not to speak up or shape-shifted in order to blend in. I may have appeared still to the casual observer of my chameleon-like antics but all the while I was journeying far and wide within myself. Life has become a very different adventure since the recognition of these self-limiting beliefs with their accompanying strategies and behaviors. Rather than following a map of expectation and externally defined 'reasonableness', the time has come to move forward and explore my own unique terrain.

As tempting as it is to dwell on 'what' is required and the 'where' and 'when' questions in exploring this new terrain, I simply trust myself to make up the details as I go. I continue to show up fully and choose to begin where I am in the moment. My promise to myself is to let go of my desire to retrofit my truth and simply discover it with no strings attached to the past and no set agenda for the future. My days of voyeurism are over. Living fully and writing about it as a means to discover all the different facets of experience has allowed me to live as an engaged participant in my life rather than having my nosed pressed to the glass. I have stopped reading the map and I am exploring the territory.

This exploration involves far more than embracing an emerging identity that includes 'writer'. It requires that I live my life in full color and claim publicly all the aspects of myself that I have kept tucked away. I'm betting that you know exactly what it is that I'm talking about. How much more we know ourselves to be but we continue to go along with the flow. Making small talk, being small. Hiving off aspects of our selves to fit in at work or with friends and even with our families. Living in tacit agreement that we "just won't go there".

And so we all go along in a socially induced daze that only permits microscopic conversations because we don't want to pry. Curiosity is impolite. We fear judgment. We remain locked in a dance that denies us the intimacy of ourselves and robs us of the chance reveal ourselves and become more intimate with someone else. It scares us to death. Why is that? Have we been rejected and hurt so much in our lives that we are beyond recovery? I don't believe that we are beyond recovering a sense of self for a second. I know that to reveal ourselves in a way that makes reclaiming our authenticity possible is an act of courage.

The restless genius that lives in me has led me to this place where a new beginning is possible. I have acquired many tools along the way that give me a unique perspective of the bridges that exist between science and the esoteric. I have come to realize that what we hold as fixed and real is a construct of our own perceptions of reality. When the context changes, so does our perception. My old context of success dramatically changed when I began to tune into the voice of my authentic self. Success based on an external reference is one context and the context of an inner reference point of hopes and dreams completely and irrevocably redefined my reality.

I no longer believe that there is the one and only one way to consider the world. I have become curious about what can be discovered when we take something that we think is "just how it is" and become willing to play with it and blur its edges to see what pops out. Now that I can recognize what a context is, I am noticing that it can be a lot like playing with a kaleidoscope. Make one shift and all the elements reorganize themselves into a wonderful new image. Make another adjustment and poof- a different image! I invite you to entertain the possibility that what you hold as "real" may be more malleable than you think. If you were an elephant, are you really being held back or are you living your life based on a habituated response to the tug? Be playful in considering that there may be different ways in which to consider the world. Be willing to allow yourself to step outside the clearly defined box of your current perception of reality and have a look around!

As my perceptions have shifted I can see that I have become well versed in both healing arts and human hearts in this journey from Physiotherapist to my authentic writer self. I have a deeper appreciation of the incredible power and potential that we carry in our bodies to support us in becoming much more in our lives and our evolutionary journey. We were not designed to be puny, small and fearful. We are magnificent beyond measure. We have simply forgotten it in the midst of all the illusions that hold us captive.

Based on this new vantage point I have also become convinced that each of us carries within us a wellspring of potential that lies in readiness, awaiting our discovery. It never dries up no matter how long it has been since we last drank from it. It simply is. Always present. Ever ready. It is a source of health, peace, creativity, and contentment. I believe that we deserve it and that we are designed to embody it. Anything less betrays our potential and diminishes our humanity. This notion is part of popular wisdom. Consider the phrases, "use it or lose it" and "life is not a dress rehearsal".

So what stops us once we awaken to our authentic self? Perhaps it is our fear of the unknown or a belief that we must work long and hard on ourselves, sacrifice ourselves for a larger ideal. Perhaps it is that we feel we don't deserve to live at our fullest potential. Consider the beliefs about scarcity that run our lives- not enough time, not enough money, not enough energy. It is never too late to choose differently. Once we become willing to wake up to our authenticity and embrace our wellspring of hopes, dreams and potential we must take action and choose for ourselves whether we will numb and anesthetize ourselves or if we will step boldly into the larger adventure that life offers. Not taking steps to align with our inner compass leads to consequences that impact the quality of our lives. A lack of alignment suppresses our vital flow.

If you are wondering how to excavate your authentic self after many years of not heeding its call, I urge you to pay attention to the genius of your restlessness. The restlessness may be in mind, body or spirit, but you will sense its presence. It may come disguised as the barely glimpsed thought, the recurrent dream, a fleeting sensation that escalates into a physical symptom demanding your attention. No matter how it comes to you, if you are willing to awaken, stretch and look around at your world differently, you will begin to find the trail back to something long forgotten and still present, silently waiting. Moving with the rhythm of your restlessness rather than swimming against its current sets you on the path to self-discovery.

The genius in my restless journey has also lead me into many of my fears only to discover that I am much more than the illusions that have limited my life. I have walked through my fears, felt the impact in my body and discovered that as I relax into the sensations and lay claim to them, I am able to see that fear and self-limiting beliefs are simply veils. They are constructs of my habits of thought and early learning. Until I embraced them as I began moving forward, I was held in place by the nameless. This discovery has not rendered me fearless, I simply know those sensations to be signs of life. When I pull back, the restlessness returns, prodding me to move forward into the unknown.

Uncertainty is the platform of formlessness out of which we have full reign to create. It is a playground of potential, a fertile void. It is a place to co-create with whatever we believe sources us – God, the Universe or the Higher Self. We have become so fearful of the unknown and so divorced from our inner wellspring that we continue to choose to create our lives based on the past. We repeat our history over and over again and wonder why nothing ever seems to change. We struggle to let go of our habits of thoughts and our rigid perceptions because we fear what we don't know. We have been taught not to trust ourselves and to put our unquestioning faith in the external guideposts that have been set up for us to follow. I know what it takes to break the pattern, to walk through the fear and to be transformed; to walk through the fire and discover that you possess not just a bit of potential but exponential potential to create a life that is meaningful for YOU. What it requires is unwavering faith in your inner compass, YOUR inner truth.

I don't know about you, but along the way I had learned to never trust my truth. "That is not what is really happening" is what we are told when everything in our body knows that to be untrue. Adults try to reassure us or have us participate in their own denial and before you know it, the one true voice that speaks to you, fades into the distance. Can you ever trust it? Was it ever really there? The volume is so muted that at times it seems if you are lucky enough to hear it, that it is coming from a far away place.

How freeing it has been to discover that it never really leaves us. No matter what you call it - God, Source, Higher Self - many of us can sense its presence in our lives. We want to believe that there is something more. Something more cannot show up completely in our lives until we create the space for it by being willing to stop running from the fire within us. As it begins to flow, it transforms. In its wake we are left with the space in which new signs of life can emerge. We are moved to action in our lives and as the action is sustained, flow appears. A life in flow has all the signs of vitality, freshness and renewal. All the stagnation is swept away once we are willing to release our grip. The simple act of letting go is one the most courageous and liberating things we can do. In its wake follows magic and miracles. The events in life we often attribute to luck or synchronicity begin to appear as a larger plan unfolds.

Choosing to live as a full expression of myself means that I must be willing to fully accept myself as who I am in this moment and who I am becoming. I do not need to judge my past or conform to a prescribed future. I can craft my life as a work in progress. I am certain that it will have a surprise ending! Frankly, the story of our lives is never done and yet this is how I spent many years living, enslaved by the next thing and then the thing after that, never arriving at a destination that could fulfill what I was searching for. Seeking education and credentials, career, material security, the 'right' relationships and then some kind of spiritual achievement. It was all a game with the only possible outcome being to win or lose. Now I am embracing the much larger game of life and object of that game is to keep it in play for as long as possible.

I have begun walking a different path, a labyrinth that spirals ever outward containing all the steps of my journey as circles within circles. Each new circle becomes a larger context in which to hold the previous one. Each completed circle claims and holds the territory around which the next is built. Walking this path has required lots of letting go and venturing into the unknown. In my life, just like in a labyrinth, I may not have the vantage point to see the larger pattern emerging. I simply must trust as and move forward in order to discover its beauty and mystery. Standing still leaves me with only a fixed view of the whole, only a snapshot of the total experience. Retracing my steps has taken me down paths where I trade the temporary comfort of familiarity for stasis. It is only by moving forward that I can create a different experience for myself.

This journey in my life so far has required me to become honest with myself and to take responsibility for my past, my present and my future. In sharing my story, perceptions and discoveries I can claim the fiery creation of my emerging writer-self and continue my journey into the next chapter waiting to be created in my life story. Perhaps in sharing my story, you will find something of yourself here too. I wish you well on your journey, fellow traveler.

Acting on her commitment to live a life that is a full expression of her intention, Anita Allen sold her Physiotherapy practices and created WELsprings; an Institute that reflects her firm belief in the depth of potential each person carries.

Anita is the creator of Exponential Potential™, a program experience that offers a WEL-Systems® perspective as a platform to assist participants to tap into profound personal potential in a way that fosters life affirming change.

As a Physiotherapist, Anita embraces the notion of self-regeneration and autopoiesis by incorporating The CODE Model™ in her work with clients and other healthcare practitioners.

An avid writer, Anita continues to contribute to books, websites and e-zines while she explores all that life has to offer as she follows her inner compass.

Connecting With The Genius

Theresa McKeown

At this point in my life's journey, I don't really know if my story of how it was is even true. You know how it works, stories seem to take on a life of their own and often when I'm telling mine, particularly to mySelf, what I suspect I may be telling is merely my remembrance of the last version, rather than my body's experience of the original events. A kind of retrospective revisionist tale.

It's also very easy to get sidetracked on the sub-plots. Over time, as I became more and more disconnected from myself, from my body, I'd recount a minds-eye version, a sometimes dramatic interpretation of what happened rather than how it really may have been or how it felt.

And so, for the part of me for which this story has truth, my memory is that once upon a time, it was hard work and uncomfortable. This was consistent with a set of adopted beliefs, values and attitudes I acquired; ones that are very different from those I have chosen as my own that frame my life today.

The adopted beliefs, values and attitudes were predominately based in fear and scarcity. The values I choose and re-choose today are based in trust and abundance - a transformative shift that came, and continues to flow, from my connection with The Genius of mySelf. It is that delightfully and magically simple!

Breathing and dropping into my body, I ask "How was it"? And what rises is something like "Be Good! Do as you are told, or else. Look out, be careful, try harder, not good enough, try harder still. Do not be or do any of the things you must second guess they do not like you to be, or do." Life was serious and hard work.

From a very early age, I probably felt uncomfortable, disconnected, out of place; not knowing where or what my place was much of the time. It seems to me there was a sense of being on the outside, looking in, never really being part of or accepted as. My body memories of this are feelings of cringing and tightening, accompanied by an insatiable yearning to please, to be accepted, loved, appreciated and validated by others.

And so I worked hard, studied, learned, practiced, traveled, conceived, aborted, taught, dispatched, appraised, edited, sold, served, married, divorced, strived, proved, accomplished, impressed, inquired, investigated, repressed, suppressed and cried real and imaginary tears. In between, I played, laughed and explored, periodically mindful of an almost unconscious backdrop of a requirement for vigilance - just in case.

I fed the insatiable yearnings with never enough education, accomplishment, attention, awards, trophies, adventure, alcohol, drugs, food, sex, change and movement. Always changing - interests, focus, jobs, lovers, locations, distractions, titillations – all the while moving further away, from mySelf.

I did whatever it took to ameliorate the sense of something's missing, something's not quite right, until I could no longer do it, until it became, the refrain rises in me, "like a wild fire running out of control." The words come from somewhere. I can't quite place them. It's not the Eagle's - I know that one. It's "she wondered how it ever got this crazy."

Out along my timeline, around the 40 year point, I just stopped and surrendered to I can't do this anymore. It's as if there were parts of me that decided "We ain't gonna work on

Maggie's farm no more, and if you're going to continue to do this, then you have to go on without us." Or, at least, that's how I once heard Stephen describe it about a woman whose Spirit finally refused to continue doing what she had designed for herself.

No matter how hard I cringed; no matter how much sheer will I exerted to force me through the daily motions of my life's routine, the "wildfire out of control" was not containable. It wouldn't be doused by any of the retardants I'd thrown at it for years, and when it began to move in its full blazing power, it scared the hell out of me. I was losing control of what I was clinging to as the representation of who I am. All of which was an illusion, anyway. The illusion, that is, of ever being in control. Or that what I was clinging to actually was who I am. But don't let me get ahead of mySelf.

Succumbing to the Fire, letting it burn and walking through the blaze is, according to the mystics, the pathway to transformation. Alchemic magic strips away the impurities, the Phoenix rises from the ashes and what is left is the pure element, the real deal. I'd heard it, read about it, but how did one actually do it?

Surrendering was not all that difficult, in hindsight. The clutching and desperately hanging on just before the point of letting go was very difficult. Knowing that I could no longer hang on to the known, when I let go and took the leap of faith into the unknown, I experienced mostly relief.

And so began the process, for that is what it has been, an unfolding process rather than a series of discrete events, in the most alive and fascinating period of my life. It began with me thinking I needed to learn and understand more about mySelf, to examine what I was doing or needed to do, to get smarter.

For a few years I did just that, diving into any personal growth opportunity that came by - psychoanalysis, the Forum, rehab, natural healing, bodywork, nutrition, reiki, meditation, esoteric studies, monastic and yogic retreats. Self-help material careened off shelves at me. For about five years, I was celibate, literally, focusing my energy and attention with committed intent on The Inquiry. Celibate that is, until I drove into orchard country one summer and had an encounter with a peach farmer - like a heroine in a D.H. Lawrence novel. But that's just one of those distracting sub-plots.

As we know, from committed intention and focused attention, flow synchronicity and serendipity. Kindred spirits, maestras, opportunities, signs, convincers, insights and genius were abundant. I received tangible evidence that the grace and bounty of the Universe are available to me, as they are to each of all of us. And the fundamental prerequisites were spiritual awakening, mind-body connection and letting go.

During that period, I made a pact with a yogini friend, as she was dying, that the shared experience of her passing would irrevocably alter my life. One winter night, as I contemplated the re-design of my life, I declared and wrote "I am an independent business woman, connected with mySelf, facilitating personal and organisational change, from a base in Canada, with clients in various parts of the world."

That spring, I resigned from a career that offered security, money and ego gratification but had decreasing intrinsic value to me. My objective was to free up time and energy to devote to The Inquiry as I had a sense of urgency about discovering why I am here.

It was no longer about learning - it was about how I am *being*, moment by moment; how I am living my life as a demonstration of who I am. I choose to trust that what I need will come, and when I am less than 100% congruent with my stated belief, I just remind mySelf, over and over again, that I believe it.

As the re-design of my life unfolded, a serendipitous Mexican gift presented itself, a place where I've spent time each winter leading exercise classes and sharing neuro-linguistic programming (NLP) and trance-formation experiences. It represents an opportunity to practise all the things I am - spontaneous, authentic, inspiring, fun, curious and connected with mySelf and other kindred spirits.

At the same time, my business in Canada has sustained me, evolved and diversified into areas consistent with my interests and values. When I first heard of the logical levels in NLP, the part of me that had already known about this just smiled when I acknowledged what I'd done. That winter night, I had declared and held an Identity for mySelf and, then over time, alignment occurred at the other levels of spirit, beliefs, values, attitudes, strategy, behaviour and environment.

It is clear to me that what I value most is connection - to mySelf, to those I love and to kindred spirits who show up on my Path. My committed intention is to connect, tell mySelf the truth and align my behaviour accordingly and, from this intention, insights unfold as to how to actually do it.

One of my constant companions is my pendulum, a biofeedback device I use to support my connection with mySelf and to guide my decision making. I make very few decisions without deliberately consulting my body - my unconscious mind. When I ask "do you want to do this" and I get a "no" signal, I pay attention to this very unconscious response, even if there are other aspects of me that seem to want to do it and can get very loud about being heard.

Perhaps it was because of my desire for this deep connection that trance resonated with me from the moment I first began to explore hypnosis. I figure some of us who were or saw or read about the 'flower children' of the 60s and 70s know that what we sought in drugs, sex and rock and roll is available through trance - the connection with ourselves and others, the going inside, focused or heightened awareness, clarity and the relaxation or relief from our daily rhythms.

And as trance is a naturally occurring state, when we deliberately induce it, we are merely utilising something we already do, easily and effortlessly. We all know the driving trance - the "how did I get here" moment at the end of the drive to work. Or how about the TV trance, the gardening trance or, perhaps, the golf trance! When I heard a former British Open Champion describe "this eerie calmness" that he felt during the final round, I knew what he was really talking about was the uptime trance state which world class athletes are in when they are at their peak performance - when they are demonstrating their connection with Genius.

Throughout this evolving process, a very significant constant is that I have always been very physically active, initially involved in team sports as a young woman and later as a fitness instructor interested in aerobics, cycling, hiking and yoga.

The Observer began to notice, however, that the longstanding connection the 'I' had with its 'body' was changing. It was becoming less about physical prowess and competition, and more about the body being a way to really check on, and connect with, how things were going. Particularly once I stopped anesthetizing my body, I became aware of the areas where I held 'tension' and how much stuff was always going on, particularly in the area of my gut - my hara, third chakra, power centre - the energetic element of which is Fire.

I'd had an awareness of this gut area activity for a long time and my customary reaction had been to name it, and then to satiate, dull or fill it, with whatever it took. And as I paid closer attention to the sensations that were almost always there, it began to dawn on me that the distinctions I had been making may have been artificial and intellectually based.

My mind often hadn't really known what was going on down there, in my body. It all felt pretty much the same - I just added an interpretive overlay to the physical sensations, sometimes calling them nervousness, other times calling them excitement, hunger, anxiety, sadness or whatever. My mind would make up a story based on the context within which the sensations occurred or as justification for actions I wished to take to satisfy the cravings, yearnings, feelings or sensations.

This insight into how it really works was the point at which my life changed significantly, exponentially. Up to that point, I had been pursuing and experiencing incremental change, mostly at the level of environment, behaviour and strategies. Once I grasped that it was about spiritual awakening and that access to MySelf - my Spirit - was through my body, quantum shifts began to occur.

This marked the end, literally and figuratively, of the dissociation from mySelf. Having shifted to the language of energy, being very curious about the energy moving in my body, I not only allow it to move, I enthusiastically invite it to move.

Drop into my body; breathe, let the energy move and speak my truth. That is my mantra today - the WEL-Systems® paradigm. As my body calibrates for truth and congruence, I pay attention and remind myself that the only truth I know is my own. Anything about anyone else is just something I am making up.

This doesn't mean I don't get sucked into judging and doing other people's inventories. Nor does it mean I don't feel jealous, competitive, insecure, angry, righteous or any other nominalisation I call the sensations. All it means is that I, more often and sooner, recognize and then choose to stop or continue doing whatever it is. When I feel less than safe or confident or certain, I practise accepting the energy states and not letting them stop me from behaviour that is consistent with whom I choose to be. Distinguishing between my energy states and my action strategies, I can choose when to act out my reactions or just let my body metabolise the associated energy.

I've learned about trance logic – the ability to accept seemingly contradictory states, without conflict - which means there is more ambivalence and less mutual exclusivity in my world these days. I am generous and covetous. I am inclusive and exclusive. I am committed and don't give a shit. And isn't it great that I can be all those things at the same time? There is space in me, for me to be all the things I am without needing to eradicate or eliminate those aspects of myself I used to be less than fond of.

I practise letting the Fire energy flow when it starts to move in me and I remind mySelf the same energy that feeds my rage also feeds my power, passion and creativity. As I invite the energy to move, I'm mindful of sometimes just breathing; of not having to say or do anything. And other times, particularly in response to other peoples' Fire energy, I let them see and experience mine, as Fire energy recognizes itself in another. I've practised saying "no", and when pressed on "why not", I've mastered saying "because I don't want to".

I pay attention to the incessant internal dialogue I create and I'm able, more often and sooner, to identify that which comes from my authentic self and that which is a product of others. I hold as a belief that I can be whomever I choose and have any life I want – I am the designer and creator – and all I really have to do is pay attention. And in moments when I am feeling less than 100% congruent with this belief, I sometimes remember to remind myself that all I need do is keep choosing and re-choosing it as my belief.

I believe truths and insights will show up, and so they do - although it sometimes takes a while for me to see them. Last spring, for three days, a robin bashed into my window from dawn to dusk. My initial reaction was annoyance. Then I began to get very curious, asking mySelf "What is this really about? If I create the holodeck upon which this robin has shown up, what are the learnings in this for me? What is trying to get my attention by bashing into the pane/pain"?

My mind told me perhaps this robin has fallen in love with the bird it thinks it sees in the window, experiencing perfect rapport, impeccable mirroring or matching of each other's every movement, all those almost imperceptible little head jerks. And so I had to ask myself "How often am I attracted to, do I fall in love with my own construct, based on a perception, an image I hold that is not even what is really happening?"

When I began to consider the possibility that the robin might be defending its turf, fighting off threats, I asked myself "How often am I fighting with or defending myself from my own constructs, things that are not even real?"

And so, I pay attention to my constructs and the beliefs or criteria upon which they are based. In listening for others' truths, and in speaking mine, perhaps I will manifest more of that which is congruent with my truths. One of these is that I construct and attract experiences and learnings to support mySelf, in the same way The Genius supports me.

He showed up again today - Einstein, that is - and I was so delighted. I thanked him for reminding me of what he'd first revealed to me when I was doing hypnosis trainers training, pursuing my most inspired and inspiring passion. Even now, as I think and write about the experience, revivifying how it felt, what he sounded like, the energy moves in my body. I call it poignant delight and gratitude at the very tangible evidence of my connection with mySelf. And each time he reappears on my holodeck, all the power and magnificence of our first encounter is recreated and re-anchored, which to me means that I am continually recreating his appearance to me, for me and by me. How ingenious is that?

So today, as I prepared to finish writing this, he appeared in an early morning conversation with a friend who did not know about my connection to The Genius; nor that I had been contemplating what my contribution to you might be, as you are reading this now. Then it came to me in a flash, as the Observer that I am was witnessing me reminding mySelf of my first encounter with The Genius.

> *There is a telephone call for me. I take it and discover - incredulous, amazed and honoured - that Einstein is calling me. And he says "You do not have to worry about anything. I am with you and will always be. When you are at the front of trance training rooms or wherever else you are, whatever you are doing, I am there."*

Profoundly moved by the dream, I awaken and I thank mySelf for delighting and surprising me with the message. Now each time he appears, in whatever form, I interpret it as tangible evidence that I am influencing the quantum field. And I do so because when I set an intention, I request, and then watch for, evidence that my intention is unfolding in a way that delights and surprises me. Sometimes when insights or great ideas appear, I wonder if they have come because I am creating my life, day by day, as The Genius.

So perhaps in a similar way, my contribution to you may be to remind you that wherever you are, whatever you are doing, The Genius You Already Are is alive… inside of you… yearning and waiting to connect with you, whenever you are ready. And all you need do is breathe, drop into your body, let the energy move and connect with your truth. Then, when you are delighted and surprised by evidence of the connection, you might even say - with your real or your imaginary voice - a very grateful "thank you" to yourSelf.

A curious iconoclast, Theresa McKeown facilitates experiences that alter people's lives and workplaces. Her international consulting, mentoring and training business is based in the Ottawa Valley and, in the winter, in Mexico. As a management consultant, Theresa specializes in organizational design, change management, strategic communication and executive mentoring.

An NLP Master Practitioner and a certified Hypnosis Master Trainer, she is inspired by trance-formation and connection. A YWCA certified fitness instructor for more than 20 years, her mind-body practices include hiking, aerobics and yoga, as well as meditation, bodywork and breathing techniques.

Connecting With The Genius

Embracing the Fire Within

Carole MacInnis

Where do I begin with the story of my own evolution? Looking back, I realize that from an external perspective, I had accomplished a lot. I was a Ph.D. tenured professor with extensive involvement in non-profit work, as well as the mother of three amazing young men. While my life was busy and full of projects, there seemed to be something missing. And as good as it was, I found that my life was becoming more and more defined by struggle.

I decided to leave the university environment to open a retreat centre for groups and individuals. Most people thought this was a foolish decision as I had left a job which had great benefits and guaranteed a good retirement. While I loved teaching and research, much of what was involved in the university culture was about power and small 'p' politics.

For someone who believes in the power of relationship in work, working in an environment where trust was scarce was not sustaining me. The 'publish or perish' environment, which created jealousy among peers, was a place where speaking out could mean that colleagues would not speak to you for months – and those same colleagues were involved in your peer review. It had become a difficult place for me to build meaningful relationships.

I now know that I was in a constant state of trying to perform according to other people's standards. I also know that some of my most profound work was outside the academy's framework. More and more, I came to recognize that I did not feel I belonged. So with all the enthusiasm of a much younger woman, I began a new adventure, this time (as it turns out) with most of my family involved.

I had a desire to create a nurturing environment that would support others in doing the kind of work which I felt was needed in the world. Being on the edge of burnout, and watching others do the same, I felt that if the right environment were created that could help renew and refresh people, I would continue to make a difference in a way that was also meaningful to me.

Prior to leaving the university, I had dreamed of a place by the ocean where a centre could be built. At first, it was just a fantasy. As I found myself talking about this to others more and more, it began to seem possible. It was going to require a leap from what traditionally felt secure for me. From my very early years, it had always been important for me to be financially independent. This decision to move away from my secure, sure-thing job to start a business with my husband/partner brought up many of my old insecurities.

After finding the courage to make the leap into what was essentially unknown territory, I began what would be one of the most major growth journeys of my life. Never having been involved in a business before - let alone a family business! – my life was full of constant challenges. My belief was that shared ownership of a business of this nature would help assure its success. So my partner and I began to work together on the project.

In our naiveté, we managed to accomplish a great deal: financing the project, designing and building most of the facility, etc. While we went forward with much dedication, everything seemed a struggle. Two steps forward and one back. While we were making progress, the project was still taking its toll on us. Development costs were over budget and, like many small businesses, we overestimated our initial revenues as well.

Money became a big focus for me; we were undercapitalized and there was not enough cash flow being generated by the business to sustain it. As a result, much of my energy and creativity went toward the financial arrangements of the business. This was an interesting position for me. I have always had an abundance filter when it came to money so to have so much energy focused on the day to day money issues was new to me.

The co-management relationship with my partner was also stressful. We learned that we had different core beliefs about management and leadership; and we learned that they were not compatible. We spent a great deal of time trying to convince each other of our positions which only succeeded in creating stress on both our personal and business relationship.

The depth of our belief and our passion for the project made our lack of agreement even more frustrating. I was terrified. My life seemed to be in chaos. I began to question my decision to leave my university career behind. When I would get too frustrated with our attempts to work together, I would get involved in outside projects related to my earlier work. I even went back to teaching for a while, first on a part-time level and then on a more full-time basis at a nearby university. While this would bring in some monetary rewards, it was clearly not where my heart was. So, we would try again.

Whenever I found myself in conflict with my partner over the direction of or specific details in the business, I would start to move back to what was known to me; trying to hold on to my previous life in order to feel more secure and to not threaten the relationship. I loved my husband and did not want us to be split apart. So when I saw no other way, I swallowed much of my frustration and sadness, as I am sure my partner did as well.

The difficulties we were experiencing from our having chosen co-leadership was upsetting to me on several fronts. One was my hope that we could develop this dream as a partnership. Another – and the most significant - was my belief that a cooperative effort between us would result in so much more than either one of us individually could achieve. My partner held a different belief which was based on more established business models. Much of what he had read in the field of management stated that it was impossible to have a co-management situation. So the dance continued.

Many of our family, friends and staff watched as we both began to deteriorate, emotionally and physically. Our anger grew in what became a situation where neither one of us could manifest our vision. Of course, this had a significant and visible impact on the business and so the struggle continued. We would achieve one victory which would be followed by another challenge. While the general movement was forward, it began to take its toll on all of us.

Much of my earlier academic work had involved examining the need for a paradigm shift in education. My belief focused on a more holistic approach to education which I felt was essential to the learning process and the development of the individual. While I believed it was also true in a business situation, we seemed to be stuck in a reductionistic approach. Margaret Wheatley, in her book Leadership and the New Science: Discovering Order in a Chaotic World, describes how problems are viewed from a Newtonian world view:

> We treat a problematic organization as if it was a machine that had broken down. We use reductionism to diagnose the problem; we expect to find a simple, singular cause for our woes. We sift through all the possible causes of failure, searching for that one broken part – a bad manager, a dysfunctional team, a poor business unit. To repair the organization, all we need to do is replace the faulty part and gear back up to operate at predetermined performance levels. (1999, p. 138)

With our relationship hanging by a thin thread, the business still not profitable and now two of our three sons involved in the business as well, I became sick. I had previously been diagnosed with a chronic form of cancer called marginal cell splenic lymphoma. Initially, this condition had stabilized after my leaving the university. After several years of our attempts to work as co- managers, my white blood cell counts began to get higher and my spleen larger. It became clear that I would have to have my spleen removed. Not only would this not cure the cancer, it would remove an important part of my immune system.

Of course, the spleen is in the area of the third chakra. What I was later to learn is that the third chakra is the power chakra. It is not surprising that this is where disease would develop in my body. Louise LeBrun describes the function of the third chakra in her book, <u>Phoenix Rising: The Freeing of Human Potential.</u>

> The third chakra, the Power chakra, is the center of the ability to take action. It is from this area that I experience the energy that powers my capacity to take action on my own behalf. The fuel (and the element) is fire, combustible and resulting in movement, either slow (embers) or rapid explosions. (2003, p.70)

It was in this moment that I began my journey into WEL-Systems®. With an extensive background as a psychologist and an educator, I was not prepared for the profound effect this new way of understanding the world would have on me.

After experiencing a WEL-Systems weekend program, I went into the hospital for my operation. Surprisingly, both the surgery and my recovery went extremely well. As a matter of fact, my doctors were amazed at how well I was recovering. At this point, I really knew very little as to why I was able to go through this experience with such peace of mind. I had always felt that there was something to be learned from my illness. Prior to my WEL-Systems experience, I had read numerous books related to healing and had participated in different programs to become more self-aware and yet, I would inevitably find myself still stuck in the same patterns. During my recovery, I made a commitment to myself to find a way to move forward in my life with more joy.

Five months later, I stepped into a week-long program which would change my life: a program called *Igniting the Self* offered by The WEL-Systems Institute. Taking a week in which the total focus was on my growth - not from an intellectual perspective (I already knew how to do that exceptionally well!) but as an exploration of the information my body carried - created the space in which change could occur. That week would bring a complete pattern break for me.

I began to understand that my body had long been trying to communicate to me what was wrong in my life. Through fear and a deep cultural indoctrination, I had been unwilling to release the power that was so much a part of me. Although people would frequently perceive me to be calm, successful and caring, inside a rage was growing.

Much of my work had been in the areas of supporting people who I perceived as vulnerable when it came to issues of power. I was comfortable in being a champion for others and speaking out against injustice, and more than once put my job on the line to take a stance. Yet, I was not comfortable in expressing my own power, despite my beliefs regarding equity and my willingness to fight for others. I began to realize that I still had some fears about power that were residual from my childhood.

While I felt that I had already deconstructed my cultural upbringing, it was becoming clear that there were still threads of it operating in my life, especially when it came to my life partner and our new adventure. We bring our family histories with us into all work settings; but in a family business, these histories are enmeshed with stories told from many perspectives. Since ours was primarily a family business, family relationships were playing a significant part in the development of the business.

A family business presents the ultimate challenge when dealing with the impact of cultural upbringing. We each are operating with our own unique family system in the background as we are running the business, and at the same time living together as a family. The rules of engagement within a family (whether perceived or real) are the subtext for each interaction. If you add to that each individual's beliefs about business, you have a web of complexity that is dazzling!

My partner and I have three sons, all of whom have played some part in the family business. As well, our two daughters-in-law work in the business. The talent and skills represented by all the family members was not only complimentary but each was essential to the success of the business. And in the midst of it all, I began to realize that I brought many of my old filters with me while engaging in the family business. I would discover that my own family system history was alive and well.

I grew up in the southern part of the United States where men and women had a particular set of rules for engagement. From the time I was a young child, I learned that you were not to challenge men directly. My mother and other significant women in my life modeled that the only safe way to have a voice was to manipulate in an indirect way. The number one rule was that men were always made to look good.

The message I received was that direct communication and visibility had negative consequences. This was reinforced in my professional life as well: when women were put in positions of power, everything was fine until they challenged the status quo. The consequences of speaking out were often that they would loose their position or simply be pushed aside.

The message was that as long as the women walked the party line, they were safe. So I learned again that power was dangerous as it would be a threat to others. Some would even suggest that a woman who stood in her own power was unfeminine. (It's interesting to notice who was defining what was feminine.) To make changes, I learned that you had to carefully watch how you positioned yourself. The overall effect of this was that the genius, that we as women had to bring to the table, fell silent.

Just when I felt I had freed myself from this limited view of women by owning my own business, the pattern seemed to be repeating itself. Even though I held up a great deal of the infrastructure and had many talents to bring to the situation, people from the outside world repeatedly would see the business as my husband's business. And if not my husband, then my son would be identified by others as the business owner/leader.

Coming from a history of identifying and confronting equity issues in my previous work, I was outraged! Part of me felt it was just another case of gender inequity. It was a situation which I felt helpless to remedy. I blamed my husband for not making it clearer to others. I felt he should step aside and give me a chance to be on committees representing the business. After all, I had lots of experience in working with others in a committee structure. I found myself falling into a victim mentality.

What I began to realize as I was moving into a different level of self-awareness, is that my cultural upbringing of being invisible - because being visible was dangerous - was still with me. People were not seeing me because I was not allowing myself to be seen. My close friends and my family knew me, and the strength of my intentions as well as my talents, but I was not letting other people know who I was.

I had learned to mask my own potential when it came to others. I began to realize I was the one who would not step into my own power for fear of perceived consequences which were based on early history. What once was an intelligent response (to not be seen) was no longer serving me. My intellect knew that and at a cellular level, I still held this childhood belief. I needed to let this fear move through my body and out, making room for new information – and a more powerful way of being.

Candace Pert in her book entitled <u>Molecules of Emotion</u> describes the link between experience and biology. She refers to the hypothalamic-pituitary-adrenal axis.

> "The hypothalamus is part of the emotional brain, the limbic system, and its neurons have axons that extend into the pituitary gland, which sits below it. These axons secrete a neuropeptide called CRF – cortical releasing factor – which controls the release of another informational substance... Adrenaline is what causes the fight or flight alarm response, which is the body's natural unconscious reaction to threats either real or imagined... We could say that CRF is the peptide of negative expectations, since it may have been stimulated by negative experiences in childhood. (2003 pgs. 269-270).

Dr. Pert explains that feelings get retained in the memory not only in the brain but at the cellular level. The abuse I experienced as a child was still stored in my cells, alerting my body that I was in danger. As an adult, this unconscious belief was still having an impact on my willingness to claim my own power and the magnificence of who I had become. Once the emotion was triggered and the Fire/Power which had been trapped moved through me, my life changed. Years of behavior patterns were released in only minutes by simply breathing. How could it be so simple?

Louise LeBrun in her book *Fully Alive From 9 to 5* explains the amazing power of the breath and its capacity to create movement that heals.

> When you allow your breath to go deeper into the body, there is a corresponding opening or expansion of the body that invites movement at deeper levels of awareness. Things that you had long ago tucked far away come to life once again. You begin to notice things you've not noticed before. You can no longer ignore things that you long ago filed and often struggle to forget.
>
> When we begin to take breathing - which is a naturally occurring process of the body that generally occurs out of conscious awareness - and we bring it into conscious awareness, it can become a powerful tool for profound change. (LeBrun 1999, p. 129)

By letting emotions - which Louise calls energy or information - move through me by breathing deeply, I discovered many things about myself. I have learned so much about how we construct our world. Choosing to be visible and stepping into the power that is me, has had profound effects on me and those around me.

My partner and I have agreed to go after our separate but connected passions. I have taken on the leadership of our business, Oceanstone Inn and Cottages. Many of my beliefs about leadership and collaborative effort are being realized. The three businesses that are part of Oceanstone - the inn and cottages, the restaurant and the message therapy studio - are expanding beyond any of our wildest expectations. We have developed a lot of fans and most of our new guests are now coming as guest referrals. We have had to change our infrastructure to accommodate the increase in business.

What has changed? My willingness to speak my truth and to be the leader that I know I am. My focus for the business rests firmly in my commitment to supporting the growth of the other people on our team, many of whom are family. My vision for Oceanstone is that it will play a part in changing the world; to be a place where spirit is embraced and individuals are supported on their journey to be the magnificent creators that they are. My days are full of meaningful work with people I love and enjoy. As we create the space for everyone to grow, our team is able to move at an accelerated pace that is beyond everyone's expectation. We are spending time at the Identity Level of the business, exploring who each of the business units is individually and who we are collectively. We all have big intentions and are committed to our shared desire to make a unique contribution to the world. Seeing people grow as individuals and watching their brilliance unleashed is life sustaining.

As for my husband, he is working at the provincial level on expanding our vision to an even broader audience. Since we have changed our pattern of being stuck in a blaming mentality, he has written two books and is working on his third. His own life and vision are moving at a pace that seems unbelievable to him as well.

Our relationship has been through much change in these few months. We find ourselves feeling fortunate that we are in each other's lives. At one point in this journey, I was afraid our relationship would not survive the changes. I was so fearful. I loved him and did not want to lose him from my life. Now I know it is possible for me to have my life, for him to have his and for us – together - to create a relationship that not only is grounded in the past that we share but one that is also full of unfolding potential for our future.

Of course, there are times when we still disagree but there is more respect and understanding in our interactions; more desire to understand each other. As I discover how to make my thoughts and ideas more visible, we are able to communicate with greater depth and clarity. Before, we spent much of our time in defending our positions. Now, we accept our differences. We celebrated our 30th anniversary this year and found our way back to ourselves and to each other.

The following quote from Margaret Wheatley's book, Leadership and the New Science, best describes where I find myself these days in my relationship with others:

> As we engage in this process of exploring diverse interpretations and learning to observe our patterns, oftentimes we discover a unifying energy that makes the work of change possible. If we discover an issue whose significance we share with others, those others are transformed into colleagues. If we recognize a shared sense of injustice or a common dream, magical things happen to people. Past hurts and negative histories get left behind. People step forward to work together…The call of the problem sounds louder than past grievances or our fears of failure. We have found something important to work on, and because we want to make a difference, we figure out how to do the work, together. (1999 pg. 149)

When I think of how long I have lived with a fear of my own power; and how much time I have wasted in repeating the same patterns, I am amazed at how much simpler life is now - not to mention how much more joyful! Every day brings new possibilities and new adventures. I know that what made the difference was my willingness to claim the Fire that is part of me instead of trying to mask it. One of the benefits in claiming my Fire is that all the energy that was used to keep it from moving now is available to me to be used in more constructive ways. One of the myths that I was brought up with is that success comes from hard work and struggle. I now know that success can be achieved by clarity of intention and a willingness to just be who I am.

As I let this information move through my body and not just my mind, I realized that it was safe to be seen and express the tremendous power that was part of me. I was able to be more visible. By being more visible, I became the invitation for others to be more visible as well. It is amazing how contagious you become.

I have friends who have noticed the difference in me who are curious about what body of knowledge could have such an impact. Several of them have become involved in the programs given by The WEL-Systems Institute and are beginning to experience change in their own lives. Oceanstone, as a company, is committed to a shared model of leadership. The members of the management team have attended several workshops given by Gwen McCauley on the Seven Logical Levels as described in Louise LeBrun's book <u>Fully Alive From 9 to 5!</u> Our staff meetings have been transformed; we always seem to accomplish more than we set out to do. If we are stuck, we immediately move up to a higher level of thinking to expand our potential.

Decisions are made with ease as all listen with respect to the opinions of others. We are learning that we need to engage with each other and "support one another as the true inventors that we are" (Wheatley 1999, pg. 9). We have even begun to do our staff interviewing using the Seven Logical Levels. The interviewee learns as much about us as we do about them. We are clear about the kind of people we hope to attract to manifest our vision. Our new staff realize this is not just another job but one in which they are joining with us to create a special place where people matter. All of this happened in a matter on *months* in a world where most organizational change takes years.

As I move forward with my life and my business, I cannot predict where it will go. Nor do I want to try. By opening and embracing the opportunities that present themselves in my life, I have learned that I can be comfortable in the 'not knowing'. Why would I want to limit myself to what I can envision? By having the courage to be visible and by letting the Fire within me move, I know that I am ready for what awaits.

I am ready to be the visionary and the leader that I was born to be.

Carole MacInnis, Ph.D. is an educator and psychologist with twenty years of experience as a university professor and more than thirty years experience as a psychologist. She is presently the owner and CEO of Oceanstone, a facility dedicated to supporting individuals and groups by providing a village-like atmosphere in a seaside location which includes accommodation, dining and massage therapy services. Whether the guests are staying at Oceanstone on a holiday, for programs or for group retreats, the staff is committed to providing the service that supports the uniqueness of each individual.

References

LeBrun, Louise (2003) <u>Phoenix Rising: The Freeing of Human Potential. 2nd Edition</u>. Ottawa, Ontario: WEL-Systems Institute.

LeBrun, Louise (1999) <u>Fully Alive From 9 to 5: Creating Work Environments that Invite Health, Humor, Compassion and Truth</u>. Ottawa, Ontario: Partner's in Renewal Inc. WEL-Systems Institute.

Pert, Candace (2003) <u>Molecules of Emotion</u>. New York: Scribner.

Wheatley, Margaret J. (1999) <u>Leadership and the New Science: Discovering Order in a Chaotic World. 2nd Edition</u>. San Francisco: Berrett-Koehler Publishers.

Embracing the Fire Within

Between Caterpillar and Butterfly

Dominique Dennery

In the beginning

I came into the world with no hair; bald as a Buddha and just as round. I was given a man's name, despite evidence to the contrary. That I was born a girl was further proof of my mother's inadequacy as a woman in the eyes of my father and his clan. I was the firstborn, in a culture where the first boy is a source of great pride and girls only servants to their needs.

It was both a curse and a blessing that I turned out to be a pretty child with soft black curls. My early childhood memories carry mixed messages of unwanted attention and abandonment; pretty dresses and emotional neglect - a recipe that eventually shaped me into a woman eager to please; a vessel, a conduit for the will of another.

I wasn't always compliant. I remember my chubby two-year-old body crackling with energy, shaking with fury, screaming "No!" My mother tells the story of me stomping and trashing in the mud-filled streets of my native Port-au-Prince in the Shirley Temple dresses she made for me. Horse manure, human waste, rotting fruit, it made no difference when the Fire moved. To my great chagrin, I had been given a baby sister. When pouting was ineffective, tantrums became the fallback position as I closed my eyes to my mother's weary expression.

Then one day, my parents left. We were taken into the care of a woman managing a boarding house for children of Haitians studying abroad. My life became discipline without a trace of affection; a cold desert where my sister started to suffocate, developing pneumonia. I deadened myself to any feelings as I was held down and abused, living a nightmare but told with sugar-coated words that it was good for me. Such a wilful child, transformed in a matter of months into a shell. I became withdrawn and sullen. "Moudongue" was the Creole expression that became my new identity, replacing the Firebrand Domino.

The memories of that time only came back to me in Technicolor some months ago. Before, I had explored with a psychiatrist, a Jungian analyst, group therapy and a few New Age experiments, the experience of early childhood abandonment, never suspecting that it was a screen for abuse. The memories were locked in my adult body: pockets of information, just waiting to be released. For decades, I was in shut down mode, slightly detached from my own life. My head led the way, the body seen only as an appendage full of blood, sweat and tears; an enemy that could not be trusted.

When I was almost 16, I surrendered to the first adult male who showered me with attention, staying with him for over 30 years. He protected me from all others and from myself, as I was courted from afar by admirers - safe from predators and my own Fire, a married woman at 21. I cringe when I recall my life as a young woman - waiting for my life to begin; waiting to be pulled out of my dull existence, reading romance novels despite an advanced education; preparing elaborate dinner parties for people I didn't like; changing and redecorating houses, and spending heedlessly on designer clothing, shaping myself to please.

My life was so empty; I decided to have a child. I was almost 28 when my baby was born. During the pregnancy, I renewed acquaintances with my body. I felt incredibly powerful. My belly was growing, my ankles were swelling and I was happily huffing and puffing until the last day. For these 9 months, I inhabited my body, in the good company of my son. I had blood, skin, organs, and bones. I was a breathing, rolling, sweating organism. The intensity of the birth was almost unbearable. (Actually, it was unbearable, as the Obstetrician decided I was to have a natural childbirth with no epidural).

And when I saw his face…. For six months, I relished the intimate contact; the smell and feel of my baby, his downy hair and pudgy thighs. He had such an appetite for life, such peals of laughter, and such a contagious sense of discovery. But eventually, I went back to mind-numbing work in the civil service. I fled my child, repeating the cycle of abandonment and absentee parent I had grown up with. I sank into a depression, feeling the physical pain of a life from which I was absent. My system started to collapse: back pains, stomach spasms, throat aches, bronchitis, pneumonia, and ovarian cysts. I was slowly turning to cinder as resentment ate me alive.

My marriage became a jail term. All my Fire was directed at the man I perceived as my jailer. He, 'the source of all evil', became the subject of endless conversations with girlfriends with the same complaints. We wallowed in our misery, never once envisioning a life for ourselves as independent souls. No, it was easier to play victim and talk about all the reasons why we couldn't leave… yet. Life became smaller and smaller, as I grew addicted to spending, grooming, work. I buried myself in work, first climbing the corporate ladder, then, in my own business striving to excel, surpass, and succeed where few other women of colour had gone before.

It all came crashing down over a period of half a dozen years of exposure to notions that changed my life. Many of these notions - such as the power of breath and centres of energy or chakras - are millennium old. The notion of spirituality and a connection to something bigger than your physical self has always existed. Somewhat more recent are the notions of the power of intention, and the ability to shape your life. Am I simply mindlessly manifesting what I already know or am I manifesting what I want? Other notions are very recent discoveries about human beings as quantum physical beings and the human body as a bio-processor capable of processing and metabolizing more information, with more ease, than our brains ever will. There are also the wonderful discoveries about the links between manifestations in the physical world and patterns of thoughts. Together, these have shaken me out of my complacency and helped me open my eyes to the desert I have created mindlessly, as well as the powers I have to create a meaningful life.

What I know about breath and life

The most important discovery I have made is how to awaken the life force. It is so simple and yet continues to be something I must remember consciously. I know that all I have to do is let my breath flow in and out, like a wave. On the crest of that wave, the life force comes in and, curled at the bottom, thoughts come out; sometimes tears, always there is a body response that transforms. With breath comes attention and a deep awareness of the moment. If I keep my attention inside my body and let the wave move, I can profoundly change my life.

I held my breath for so many years; on lock-down inside while spinning out of control outside. When I let life in, I see more, feel more, want more and laugh more. I develop an awareness of the force animating my body, shaping me and filling me from head to toe. I open my mouth and out comes my truth - raw and full of poetry. The force moves my fingers and I become artistry in flow. To sculpt, all I have to do is breathe deeply and look at the pieces of clay with my mind's eye. My hands move of their own accord as I exhale and inhale. Shapes rush forward and the materials around me are allies in the creation. I can feel the colour and texture of warm brown skin. I can seize the Fire and shape the earth into the body of a mermaid or a child god. I am an infinite force, connected to something my intellect cannot possibly grasp. I become creator.

When I am facilitating small groups, there are many times now when I feel deeply connected to the energetic flow in the room. I breathe and shape these currents with care, helping each person touch the core of who they are within the safe boundaries I jealously guard. In large groups, the reach is wide, not deep, but the weaving and shaping often changes the nature of interactions and creates new life or awakens a collective passion.

What I know about connection to self and co-dependence

I know I stopped breathing when I was two. I know I was abused then and also later. The first experiences only come with the sounds and sights I associate with being underwater in the dark sea, drowning in pain. There were other instances in my childhood. But an army of censors stands on guard, starting with the force of my own intellect, compounded by the daily intake of guilt and shame from my catholic schooling and finally the dogma of my family system, whose members are well-known medical experts.

Over time, I lost the connection to mySelf and became another; actually, multiple others - with the secrets our common language. After the fiery two-year old, came the quiet girl child who tried hard to disappear, but never quite succeeded, growing small breasts at 8, starting puberty at 10, shaping herself into a woman by the time she was 12. I have early memories of feeling sensual pleasure at my nakedness and sensitive nipples and thighs, and being hit for how I looked some days and caressed on others.

When an eligible male claimed me at 15, I held on to him for dear life. There was little attraction at first. He was 16 years older, insecure and cynical. He ignored me when he was with his friends, pushed me away with great displays of anger, made love to me until I forgave him. I didn't care; I had found a haven. To keep myself safe, I became obedient and followed to the letter the old instruction manual about how to hold on to your man, i.e. pretend to like everything he does in bed, be pretty and pout regularly not to appear to be too pliant to his will. Step towards him, feel hurt, step back until he pursues you, then step sideways ignoring him, until you pretend to be conquered, then start to step forward, feel rejected, step back etc.... I danced the dance of co-dependence and became adept at the game of 'love' and manipulation.

As I draped layer upon layer of lies to veil the truth of my experience, life became small. There was little meaning to it all. So I smiled a lot, shopped a lot, worked more and more, and never stood still long enough to hear the softer and softer voice of my real needs. I amassed material possessions, debts, extra weight, personal trainers and designers, hangers-on, and a sense of self-importance. I had totally and utterly lost the path back to myself.

What I know about the still point

As I sit still under the cool Canadian sun, I let the sad songs rise from my soul, knowing I have nothing to fear. There are the songs of the well-meaning matrons speaking of the pain and suffering of women. When I listen, I feel despair at the 48 years I have spent mindlessly walking in the high heel shoes of false womanhood with nothing to show for it but a closet full of shrinking clothes and an aging body. When I am deaf to the old sirens' songs, I can feel the timeless wind putting joy in my sails. I remember who I am: a spiritual being on a human journey. I look outside of the confines of the world I have created and see limitless possibilities.

The effect of life rushing in and out can be jarring at times. The white lab coats call it manic-depressive, pre-menopausal swings, mid-life crisis, and medicate us. When the despair comes with spending sprees or binging, it's called addiction. Every woman knows that straying away from the well-worn path leads to a fate worse than death. But does it really? Are the other paths really full of land mines? Could our mothers' Self sacrifice have been in vain? What will women do, if they are not burning with resentment wrapped in the cloak of martyrdom?

As I follow the beat of my own drummer, the smallest things start to make me happy. For this to happen I know I need time; I need slowness of movement, I need stillness. When around me sits the desert with nothing in sight but sand, I must sift slowly to find the nuggets of gold. When I come upon an oasis, I must bathe and float on the clear water, while laughter bubbles around and inside me.

I have learned that every moment I am present to the journey of my soul, I become the invitation for more. No need to panic, although I still have moments where I run to the nearest high-end boutique or the nearest cupboard with sweets inside or the nearest urgent file. When I regain consciousness, I choose once again to continue the journey - one foot at a time - and life expands.

What I know about truth and compassion

Lying to myself has become impossible now that I know that what I create is a reflection of what I have been thinking. So if I refuse to see, I am made to see when card after card of my carefully constructed edifice crumbles, and I experience the defection of business partners, contracting issues, family feuds, acute financial woes, demanding dependents, physical malaise. In the eye of the hurricane, there is nothing but me: the only common denominator in my own life.

I have experienced moments of such profound loss that I have contemplated ending it all. Many times, during this journey, I have lost my self-esteem, lost my direction, lost my connection to self and to others. I have silently screamed in despair and wallowed in self-pity, as I faced the end of my illusions, the end of love, the end of the world as I knew it.

With the naked truth, has come compassion for my humanity. I have downgraded myself from an A+ to a D in self-hatred as I repeat after me: "Yes, I have done it again. No, I will not self-flagellate. Breathing is good, as I stand in the moment and remember who I am". I have chosen to go on with life, which means choosing to step away from the herd and risk ridicule and ostracism over the slow poison of mindlessness; over the bankruptcy of body, mind and soul.

What I know about living my life with intention

My highest intention is to express the artistry of life as I sculpt and write what has meaning for me. I come alive when I produce events that facilitate the awakening of groups and individuals. I come alive when I am in contact with restless souls looking for a path back to themselves. I come alive when I travel inside me and discover uncharted territory. I come alive when I travel the world and discover what other artists have created. If tomorrow I should get lost in the shadows again, I know how to get back the meaning of my life, guided by the light of my intention.

I don't know what kind of butterfly I will turn into as I quiver in my present state of transition. My head cannot make sense of what my senses tell me. My body has the answers, all I have to do is breathe and get out of the way when information moves through, releasing knowledge and wisdom I did not know I possessed. Then, I simply need to engage my own godforce to manifest intentionally.

I would like to end with a tale of transformation, an expression of my artistry, a legend about a woman's quest to come into her own power. I will call her Sekhmet in honour of this book.

Sekhmet: A tale of transformation

She was the first-born girl of a noble family. Her fate had been decided. She would become a servant of the Great Temple.

She was a strong-willed child and had to be broken first. The wise ones condemned her to the glass prison. The rooms were square and small and became a labyrinth where she got lost walking identical corridors, passing through identical doors. There was a way out but she was made to forget. After many years of walking slowly and hugging the walls as she looked out to the sky, the sun, the trees and the sea from inside the glass, she lost interest in the world. She was safe and protected in the vault inside. The sun was so bright outside, yet soft on the skin, inside. The sky was too big outside when only the blueness made it, inside. The trees shivered outside, when no rough breeze reached, inside. The sea roared outside, while the water trickled gently, inside. She fell asleep rocked by the silence. She grew blind, deaf, mute, slowly shrinking. She could hear distant voices calling outside, but moving was impossible and breathing required thought. She had none.

One day the storm roared. Thunder and lightning shook the glass sheets. She opened her eyes. The noise grew louder, making her catch her breath, accelerating the beat of her heart. Big flashes of hot light surrounded the house, impossible to ignore. She stood up waking from her dreamless state, wishing to feel the hard pellets of rain that were now bouncing off the ceiling. The roof was hit by a big bolt of lightning. The walls folded as they melted, turning into hot lava, then hardening to black shards. She was free! Drenched, singed, her hair turned to ashes, she was free! Her bones and sinews screaming to life, her hands shaping the hot air, Sekhmet had arisen.

She started walking, her feet blistered; her skin a tight mask. She found shelter in a cave where she shivered in the dampness. She licked water from the walls and felt no need for food. Alone, she started to ponder her life. So many years in a prison made by others to keep her in her place. So many years living within the constraints of thou shall or shall not. She had been such a good girl, obedient in all ways but one. She refused her fate as a servant of the dogma that demanded that she put her power in the service of others and abdicate her will. Her sister had followed the well-worn path after running away for a brief period. She was now prospering, no doubt, in a palace of her own. Was she happy? Her brother had married a mindless girl who had fast become a shrew, eaten by resentment. He had produced children, no doubt. Her father had let her be dragged away, while her mother had meekly turned her head. Were they still alive?

After resting, she walked on, her singed clothing turning to rags. She did not know where she was going; only that she had to get away from all she knew. She reached the sea and bathed, her raw skin burning, pain now a constant companion. Why not simply let the next wave take her away? Why not let her weight pull her to the bottom? Her tears became sobs; her sobs, screams; and her screams brought her salvation.

A horseman was riding by and came to her rescue, thinking she was drowning. She let him pull her out of the water, wrap her in cloth, take her with him. She remained mute, her eyes half closed swayed by the horses rhythm, her head on his shoulder. Fate had chosen for her. She had wanted protection from herself, and her instinct to stand alone and stubbornly choose a new path. She no longer wanted to think; to aspire to something no one else could envision. She no longer wanted to fight and risk being ostracized. She knew of no one like her. She must be wrong.

He had a domain of his own. A place which, she discovered, had many rules. She followed them, grateful to be taken care of. She had learned her lessons and stayed within the boundaries of the law. Be pretty and adorn yourself; be witty but don't think too much and never question your role. She bore him a son, a beautiful child with soft black curls. Was this the meaning of her life? But as the child grew and found other interests outside her rooms, she grew more and more restless.

She asked about trading in silks. He found her request harmless and let her dabble in commerce. She grew restless again and asked about buying properties and overseeing these. He acquiesced knowing she would lose interest quickly, which she did. He could see her changing and morphing into a woman with a strong temperament. He kept her happy in his bed, gave her just enough freedom for her to ripen into a lively companion, but never let her out of the domain.

One day he became ill. The domain was being attacked by enemies. It had started with just a few raids, but lately had turned into deeper and deeper forays into his fields and villages. He had grown overtired trying to preserve his people's way of life against the invaders. He developed a terrible fever and was hovering between life and death. His people looked for direction. Sekhmet stepped in.

Sekhmet started to discover who she was. She gave orders, fortified defenses, facilitated town halls and meetings of influential leaders. She oversaw the expenses of the treasury, sparing none to feed her people and intimidate the enemies. She negotiated alliances with other chiefs in neighboring domains, creating a web of relationships that was strong. The enemies looked to the right and to the left and saw nothing but determination to beat them. They rode towards the horizon in a cloud of dust.

All the neighboring chiefs celebrated their victory and Sekhmet's courage most of all. The convalescing Chief looked on, proud of his wife, yet feeling somewhat diminished by her accomplishments. He started to take back the power that he had only let her borrow for a while. She paced back and forth, back and forth, unable to accept that her fate would be decided one more time, unable to step back into the order of things. She started traveling and buying treasures by the armload, even taking a lover in a faraway land. Nothing could bring her peace.

The circle of wise women looked on with frowns of concern. She was being disruptive and must be stopped. No man should ever keep such a willful woman by his side.

One night, she heard thunder and saw lightning and realized she was creating it and had created it all along. She laughed and cried at the discovery that she had access to the very source of power, an unlimited source that could not be taken away. She left the domain under the cover of darkness without looking back. She took provisions for the long road ahead and a mount to carry her.

This time, her journey is taking her through the great desert where the sun burns all the shadows and leaves no place to hide. At night, she shivers in the cold stillness, feeling completely alone yet drawn to the multitude of lights in the dark sky above. Every dawn, she rides to the next shelter, moving with the slow deliberation of someone for whom the journey is as important as the destination. When she reaches an oasis, she bathes, letting go of all that she was, to find the pure essence of her being. She meets other travelers, but continues to travel alone, joyful in her discoveries, letting the tears flow freely, shouting her freedom.

No one knows what will become of Sekhmet; least of all herself. She trusts that she will know when to stop and when to move on, as she continues to roam the earth letting her strong intention guide her step.

To be continued…

Dominique Dennery is a facilitator, coach and trainer with two decades of experience facilitating transition in organizational settings. Her own life transitions were facilitated by the experience of the WEL-Systems® Institute series of programs, up to and including Catalyst and CODE Model Coach™. Her intention is to support the evolution and growth of leaders by designing and delivering programs based on the WEL-Systems body of knowledge and simultaneous discovery through artistic expression.

Dominique has a passion for the fine arts. She sculpts in clay; writes stories, songs and poetry; directs theatrical productions and produces large events using multiple media. Watch for transformational personal development programs that will integrate all of these elements into unique experiences.

Volcanoes and Fools

Gwen McCauley

This is one woman's story of claiming Fire; of moving beyond living life bound and shackled by the terror that the Fire which is the essence of me would one day run amok, destroying not only me but those around me; of discovering that that Fire is so much more than a force for destruction and betrayal: it is the force of my creativity, passion, irreverence, joie de vivre and curiosity about life and living.

I tell my story now as an invitation for you to discover something about yourself because I know that, in many ways, we are the same person. I tell my story now so that my discoveries of the beauty and bounty of Fire might inspire you to claim the Fire that you are. I tell my story in the hope that by connecting with my experiences, you will find the courage to move into those areas of your life that you are terrified to explore so that you will emerge a stronger, more vibrant, alive, awake person.

Probably a good place to start is with a dawning recognition when I was in my late 40's and early 50's that there was another way to think about those things called "emotions". Like you, I was raised in a culture that defined experiences in the body as either related to bodily functions (gas, heartburn, upset stomach, headache, etc.) or emotions (fear, hate, anger, rage, love, annoyance, etc.). Both types of body responses were associated with tons of rules: when it was permissible to have them and when it wasn't (e.g. perhaps it was more permissible to be sick within the family than out in public); what intensity was okay and what wasn't (e.g. it was okay to be annoyed at your parents but it wasn't okay to hate your parents); which were alright for a girl and which were alright for a boy (e.g. it was alright for boys to get angry but not alright for girls); who you could direct your responses at and who you couldn't (e.g. you could direct your responses at another person but not god). While each of us learned our own specific set of rules, that there were layer upon layer of rules for living is one way in which we are all the same.

Since we learned most of these rules for living when we were extremely young, they are often transparent to us: we simply don't know that they are running our lives. In some cases, they remain transparent because they align with more generally held rules in the culture. In some cases, they have assumed different faces and we can't see them for what they really are. In yet other cases, they have gone deeply underground and take a long time to unearth. And finally, in some cases we have developed strategies for only dealing with their opposite in the false belief that this somehow frees us from the original rule.

Now, in my particular case, my inability to engage my own Fire had a paradoxical twist to it. I grew up in a family where the dominant emotion that was present was, in fact, anger. And yet throughout my life, I've had an extreme struggle with 'anger'. (I use parentheses mindfully here because I no longer think of these sensory experiences in this way, but I feel the need to use this kind of terminology for those experiences because you will be familiar with it. Using parentheses is my way of using language that you'll be familiar with and reminding myself that it means something different to me now.)

For decades, I was most comfortable moving through my life with work and home as two separate realities. Work and home were two domains that seldom overlapped for me. In retrospect, I recognize that completely out of my awareness I had developed very different ways of dealing with my anger in each domain. It served me well to keep these two worlds separate. Even though I wasn't really aware of it, it allowed me to be two quite different people.

At home I was generally a very supportive and conciliatory woman. Small things might irritate me but other than a very brief flash of temper expressed as annoyance, I'd very quickly return to an up-beat, optimistic demeanor. That is, until something happened and I totally lost it. 'Losing it' for me meant that the volcano that I knew myself to be, and which I both feared and dreaded, would begin to erupt.

A core of molten rage would begin to rise up from some place deep in my belly and would be accompanied by a rapid increase in my heart rate and a surge of roaring in my ears. In an instant, I would become someone else. I would find myself screaming invective and obscenities at the top of my lungs, often startled at the degree of violence I felt even while I was feeling it. My volcanic outbursts frequently were out of all proportion to the size of the incident that precipitated them and were often accompanied with a sense of righteous indignation. Slamming a door or two as I stomped off always added some additional drama and seemed to allow some of the worst of the physical rage to be vented.

My rage was typically spewed on my husband for some sort of small offense: he'd folded the towels incorrectly – again; he'd asked me the same stupid question three times already, etc., etc. But there was one spectacular incident when I allowed my younger stepdaughter to precipitate such a violent volcanic eruption in me that it became the incident that told me it was time for me to somehow get a handle on this behaviour. While I didn't lay a finger on her, I knew that had I been physically close enough to reach her, there's a high degree of likelihood that I wouldn't have been able to control myself. I realized that I had been so enraged that I could have killed her. In fact, I realized that I was becoming all the worst aspects of my mother, a thing I'd sworn I'd never allow to happen. I actually chose to leave home for a couple of weeks at that time because I knew it wasn't safe for me to be in her presence.

I dreaded these types of outbursts and each time they occurred I swore that that was the last time. I was never going to allow myself to get that out of control again. And indeed, I'd be fine... until the next time!

The 'Me' I was at work was vastly different in the anger department. Still a very up-beat person, it felt much easier for me to speak my mind and to take a stand on issues in my work environment. I was very driven to succeed and as my career began to take off, I seemed to be able to thrive while driving harder and harder. No amount of work seemed to faze me. I could work 24 hrs without a break and produce prodigious amounts of output. In general, I maintained very positive relationships with most of the people I worked with. However, there regularly was someone with whom I bumped heads. And from time to time that someone turned out to be a boss.

Verbal skirmishes were my first line of defense as head butting began to surface. I've always been good with language and so it wasn't all that difficult for me to be able to intimidate the other person or to at least convince them that it was worth their while to give me a wide berth. When the going got really tough, my typical final resort was to get going... quite literally, I'd find myself another job.

So I never had large blow-ups at work. In fact, I very seldom ever engaged in the kinds of verbal dust-ups that I frequently witnessed colleagues engaging with one another. I felt very proud that I kept my anger under control at all times and diverted it into getting projects completed faster.

What I didn't notice about my strategies for dealing with anger in the workplace was how often I ended up selling myself short or selling myself down the river in order to get along. There were many times when I ached with loneliness because I'd be the only one at the office night after night after night. Despite how well I was doing, I didn't notice how many promotions or prime assignments I missed out on because I'd bail from a project before it completed because I couldn't stand the build-up of pressure between me and my boss.

But I was always extremely proud that the smoldering volcano I held myself to be didn't get loose very often in the workplace.

One thing that I was vaguely aware of during these decades of living (or half-living as I've since come to discover) was that there were people around me who seemed to have a different relationship to their feelings than I did. I remember being very puzzled on a regular basis that some of my friends and colleagues could readily identify a wide range of 'emotions' as they were experiencing them. When asked how they were feeling, they would respond with statements like: "I feel sad" "I feel excited" 'I feel very angry", etc. When I was asked that question, I typically responded with a summary of my thoughts about the situation. For example, if a group of us had just decided that we were going to pursue a big project and someone asked the other team members how they felt about our decision, when it came to me my typical response would be "I think what we're about to take on is really exciting and I'm glad we're pursuing it" whereas other people would respond "I feel excited that we're doing this, etc."

For a long time, I thought it was just a different way of expressing oneself. And then I began to engage some Self discovery processes based in NLP and WEL-Systems®. I very quickly discovered that I had created a huge barrier between my intellect and my experience of myself in my body. It was as if the most alive part of me was the part of me that was contained within my skull. Slowly but surely, I began to realize that I had virtually no awareness of the 'emotions' that were moving in my body unless they were the size of a tidal wave (or erupting volcano!).

Subtle 'emotional' responses such as anticipation, excitement, irritation, annoyance, consternation, indifference, hurt, lonely, dismayed, wary, forlorn, upset, anxious, lost, listless didn't seem to exist as experiences in my body. I had words for them, but those words didn't seem to connect with responses I was having in my body. My body seemed to be the place where I experienced only things like hunger, bladder pressure, nausea, back pain, shortness of breath and various types of aches, burbles and gurgles.

As I began to reconnect with my body, I started to notice that all of the emotional responses mentioned earlier, plus hundreds more, were actually occurring in my body; I had just become so divorced from it that I couldn't calibrate for their presence on an on-going basis.

So the early warning system of growing anger wasn't accessible to me. When I was irritated or annoyed by people, I simply ignored it until the response had grown so huge that it couldn't be ignored. My anger or rage would erupt, seemingly out of nowhere, and I would become a mad woman until it was spent. I also began to notice that my rules were such that it was more okay for me to be an erupting volcano at home than at work. Running away was my ace strategy when the volcano started to rumble at the office!

I also began to discover that as good as it felt once I experienced the release of the build up of pressure, it never made any real difference in my life. The outbursts would occur and I'd get back to living my life, ignoring all the early signals only to have the volcano blow again once the pressure had built to a certain threshold.

Finally, through my WEL-Systems work, I began to connect with the fact that my body was an incredibly brilliant, organic learning machine. I also discovered that every response I have is an intelligent response; and that I can access the brilliance that underlies my responses when I keep my body open and relaxed, and when I allow it to metabolize whatever information is moving in it.

These 'emotions' that I'd been busy ignoring because of all the rules I'd learned about their inappropriateness were, in fact, information moving in my body. 'Emotions' according to scientists like Candace Pert are the body's way of thinking. They are information or energy moving in tissue, releasing biochemicals and neuro-chemicals that interact with the brain.

When I began to engage with these body-based responses as information/energy of a specific frequency moving in the physical tissue of my body, I found that it was so much easier to stay present to my body's experiences. I could actually breathe and use my breathing to keep my body open and relaxed so that it could do its job of metabolizing the storehouse of information it had built up over the decades of my life. Because here's another thing I discovered: when we are children and have 'emotional' responses that are frowned on or disapproved of by the adults around us, we are encouraged to ignore them or move away from them long before the body has finished processing them. The unprocessed information from those experiences stays in our bodies, awaiting future processing. It is kind of like dumping raw data into a computer so that it can be processed at some future date and then never getting around to it.

Think about it: how many times when you were a kid were you upset about something and your body was flooded with your upset, only to be reprimanded by some well-meaning adult who said things like "You stop crying right now, young lady, or I'll give you something to cry for." We quickly learn that by holding our breath and distracting ourselves we can actually diminish the experience of 'upset'. We further learn that it is not okay for us to cry and that we better not think that anyone is going to support us when we are snotty nosed and teary-eyed.

What about those times when you were filled with rage and were venting your rage at someone else. "I hate Johnny!" you scream. "No you don't," says Mom. "You apologize to Johnny right now. You tell him you love him. You know that we don't behave like that in this family. You've really let me down". And invariably you capitulate, pressing down the hate in your body and saying that you feel something you don't. We learn from those experiences to fear certain 'emotions' because they get us in trouble; we disappoint the people we love when we give them free reign. We also learn to not trust our own bodies because they seem to betray us.

But all that stuff that never got processed hasn't gone away. It is the gift that keeps on giving until and unless you create the time and space to let your body metabolize or digest it. Psychologists are finally beginning to recognize the power of these early life experiences on our ability to live full, rich adult lives. They call the memories that our bodies carry, even if they were installed in pre-language periods, intrinsic memory. They know that your intrinsic memories (what I'd call unprocessed or un-metabolized information) impact how you live your life today. What I have discovered through WEL-Systems and processes like Quantum TLC™ is that none of us needs to be a slave to these early experiences. How you deal with those early intrinsic memories so that they are no longer directing your life is to recognize that when the information starts to move in your adult body, all you need to do is relax into it and let it move while you just breathe.

I've been startled by how easy and fast a process it can be. And my biggest challenge has turned out to be keeping my intellect out of the process. My intellect, probably like yours, has been relentlessly trained to believe that it is in charge and that its superior rationalizing process must be central to anything going on in my body.

I remember an event that occurred several weeks after I'd had an intensive program experience where I was able to process and metabolize a lot of stored information my body carried. My husband and I were standing in our family room and we were beginning to have an argument. I hadn't realized until that moment just how predictable our arguments were. It was as if every accusation and counter accusation were pre-determined. All we had to do was insert the words that were appropriate to the specific situation. But the dance steps and our specific roles were extremely predictable.

As usual, I noticed that the volcano inside of me roused quickly and the core of molten lava began to rise with great speed from deep in my belly. It had risen up to the base of my throat and I was opening my mouth to sling my typical insult back towards Greg. All of a sudden, I thought "Gwen, what are you fighting about? You don't even care about this anymore." In that split second, I knew I had a choice. I could continue with the dance which would lead very predictably to a hostile engagement, a few slammed doors and then a teary apology several hours later (with no real change in anything). Or I could respond differently. And I chose the different response.

I could feel the core of molten lava retreat and whatever words came out of my mouth were non-combative ones. In that instant, something shifted in our marriage. From that moment forward, our fights were different. Not only were they fewer, they became more like conversations where each of us was able to state our position and we were able to find a solution that worked for both of us. No more shouting, no more slamming doors, no more one person forcing their will on the other person, and no more need for compromises that left us both feeling like we'd lost.

In the years since those early experiences of having the volcanic me begin to dissipate, I've found that my sense of playfulness and my ability to laugh at myself and the world around me has increased dramatically.

I realized a while ago that I have come to enjoy living authentically as The Fool. Not like it's a role that I've adopted, but more like it authentically reflects who I am and who I'm capable of becoming in the world.

In the tarot deck, The Fool typically represents the beginning of a journey; trust in one's intuitive knowing; a willingness to look foolish to others because you are committed to your own pathway. There is a huge resonance in those metaphors for me.

As I've relaxed into my body, I am much more aware on a moment-by-moment basis of the wide range of information that moves in my body. I no longer relate to 'anger' or 'rage' as emotions. Rather I've come to see them as expressions of the Fire that I am in this world. And given that they are simply information moving in my body, there is nothing for me to fear. I engage the Fire that they present, as it surfaces, so there is no longer any for the volcano.

I've also recognized that laughter is another way that Fire expresses itself in the body. I've always been someone who laughed easily and I'm known for my large, loud belly laugh. For years, I was a bit embarrassed by my tendency to laugh loudly and easily and often felt that I laughed at inappropriate things and at inappropriate times.

As I've claimed The Fool within, I've also claimed that laughter is an essential expression of who I am in this world. I am no longer embarrassed by my propensity to laugh. In fact, much to my husband's dismay at times, I am very fond of laughing loudly at my own stupid jokes!

In claiming The Fool that I am, I've also discovered the joy of not doing serious work, seriously. As a coach and workshop facilitator, I am often in the presence of people who haven't yet discovered that we human beings are truly hilarious and hysterically funny; and my ability to see their misery 'through the lens darkly' opens many doors. I look back at many memories of life with my wacko mother and father and can now laugh at how cartoon-like much of my early upbringing was. Now this doesn't mean that I think people should be able to inflict all kinds of horrors on their children. Nor does it mean that I make light of the pain, terror, guilt and shame carried by many people due to life's experiences.

What I do know is that my ability to see the absurdity in many of these experiences often is the first step in my client's ability to reclaim their lives and let go of the impact that intrinsic memories (aka unmetabolized information) have created. I have found that my creativity as an agent of change in other people's lives has increased dramatically as I've claimed The Fool that I am.

The Fool has also become the metaphor that encompasses the growth in my artistic creativity these past few years. When I breathe and relax into my body, I produce paintings that are not only a joy to create, they sparkle because they represent the life force moving deeply through my body. My writing is richer and less stilted and seems to have a greater impact on those who read it. My friendships are more satisfying; my marriage more fulfilling. My garden has become more eclectic; my cooking less traditional and stuffy. Indeed, my entire life feels more alive, rounder and fuller than it ever has in the past. There is much less fear, much less trepidation, much less judging of myself and others, and very little need for compulsively consuming food, drink and consumer goods.

I've come to recognize that my Fire is my creativity and my passion for life. In claiming my Fire as the creative force that it is in my life, I no longer have to fear my 'anger'. 'Anger' is simply a label for one experience of Fire in my body. In allowing it to move within me, it gets expressed as art, books, articles, conversations, play and other creative endeavors. The volcano has retired permanently because it was only ever required as a vehicle for compressing and eventually venting the Fire I used to feel was inappropriate.

My invitation to you is to discover your own Fire and in doing so, to become the creative person that you can become. Whatever you hold as your limitations; whatever parts of yourself you are afraid of; whatever stories of shame and guilt you carry, I encourage you to discover how you too, can breathe into the information your body carries and digest or metabolize that information so that a new future - one you can only dream about now - can make itself available to you.

I am thrilled to be part of this exciting, new book because I know that all of the brilliant, courageous women who are telling their own story are just like you. Many have backgrounds of horrendous abuse; some have been blessed with great material wealth. But what they all share is that they hold a sense that they were capable of more than they'd ever been told was possible; and they were willing to simply put one foot in front of the other, confronting whatever had to be confronted as they made peace with their bodies and claimed the wisdom that living life had made available to them. If my story has sparked something in you, I would be honored to hear from you.

As I close this article, I am aware that there are deeper levels of Fire moving in me that are my invitation to begin to consider yet another unfolding of my potential. 'Cause here's the thing about Fire: it is never-ending in its generosity. Fire keeps beckoning us all into new futures, providing the impetus and incentive to become more of our boundless potential. The Fool that I continue to become is fueled by the Fire of curiosity… always wondering, always willing to explore what's next!

Gwen McCauley: educator, coach, author, facilitator, artist and 'employee to entrepreneur' veteran brings wit, wisdom and worldly experience to Self discovery as her clients explore life and career transitions, leadership, increased effectiveness and expanded creativity. Co-founder of the WEL-Systems® Institute, Gwen is a CODE Model Coach™ and Quantum TLC™ Facilitator. She has a BA in Anthropology and an MA in Human Systems Intervention.

Gwen wrote and published "The Alchemy of Energy – Exploring The CODE Model™" in 2004. Her second book "Splish Splash -- Painting for Personal Discovery", a primer for budding artists, is due for publication in 2006.

Volcanoes and Fools

UNLEASHED !

Noreen Mejias

This is *my* story of *my* journey to *my* awakening to *my* Fire, *my* Genius, *my* Brilliance, *my* existing potential to shape and to create *my* Business Practice, *my* Personal Life and *my* World!

I can now smile as I type these words, as I recall a time not so very long ago when there was no *my* or *me* in my life. No ownership. It was all 'Noreen'; all thought out and expressed in the third person, as if 'I' or 'me' were separate from my body. Strange, so much has shifted that I can't seem to recall, or bring to mind in this moment, any examples or phrases to write in order for me to share these former experiences with you. It would seem that they have disappeared completely from the way I now live.

I was an outside, impartial observer of mySelf, watching … watching… very detached, far removed, at a safe distance, as I observed the world in a seemingly calm, unemotional, flat, insipid manner. Watching and waiting, I kept mySelf bound and tied down, leashed and tethered, small and puny, accepting of my 'fate' and my 'lot in life'.

I have noticed that I have used and written the word 'waiting'. It is as if my body knew instinctively, even back then, that there was more. "There had to be more!" my body screamed even though my mind/intellect denied that such a remote possibility could even exist. My body 'screamed' at me in the form of persistent nose bleeds, allergies, colds and influenza, that no amount of medication or operations or doctors could seem to cure!

What 'more' was there to be had, anyway? It made no sense at all. No, it was better to dismiss the possibility and remain detached rather than get into trouble and be confused by constantly probing and picking away at something that seemed so nebulous, so vapor-like, so unattainable. And yet the brilliance of 'me', refused to be dismissed or be denied or be silenced. This is indeed the story of my 'Sekhmet Rising' and 'the restlessness of my very own inner genius'!

I breathe... I draw breath... I remember who I am. I am unleashed.

I remember where I am. I remember who I have become. I am alive, I am whole and I am once more aligned. It feels wonderful! It feels thrilling! It is exciting! The colors I observe are absolutely brilliant; they sparkle, they dance, they move. The pixels I observe through my shifted and changed perception of the world, have more depth and definition to them. It is absolutely amazing. It is absolutely astounding. It is so invigorating!

I sit at my laptop computer wondering what more I am going to write or where I should begin. I check in with my body and yes, I feel compelled to write; to start and to draw the picture. I forgive myself if this feels like rambling and I breathe in, drawing in a deep, long, soulful, replenishing breath. Standing in the 'now', (actually, I am sitting in the 'now' on the verandah of my hotel suite, looking out onto the ocean which is practically on my door step) I begin.

I am on the island of Tobago, in the Caribbean, at the Hilton Hotel; looking out onto the Atlantic Ocean and the rough waves that are roaring and crashing onto the sandy beach. The sound of the waves, for me, is quite invigorating. The roar of the ocean, in some ways, reminds me of my own voice and my own roar that I have chosen once more to reclaim as my own. I remember that I am unleashed and I no longer have to or need to ask for permission to allow my roar to be heard. I give mySelf permission to allow 'me' to burst forth onto the world stage whenever I am so moved to do so. No analysis, no self-talk, no self-deprivation: I unhesitatingly engage in life and a difference for me occurs... I become more!

This feeling of being carefree is so very unusual for me. This is the first time I have given mySelf permission to truly go on a holiday, just for me, in over twenty-five years. There is no agenda or script to follow; no course that I'm on that is part work/part free-time that I turn into a holiday; no friends, no family or relations that I feel I must visit or see. I know no one on the island and I like it that way. It feels wonderful. It feels safe. It feels absolutely decadent and adventurous. I went onto the Internet, did a little research and mindfully chose to make a reservation in a first-class hotel like the Hilton, for their three-night Spa Vacation Package. I am in a large two-room ocean-view suite with an outdoor Jacuzzi on the balcony.

I look up from my typing and notice a sailboat far off in the distance on the horizon, bobbing along, setting its sail to the wind and charting its own course and direction. I am reminded once again that I am unleashed. I have mindfully chosen to also chart my own course; to finally unfurl my wings & sails; to launch and set out once again and to mightily choose my own course and direction in life, and to steer and channel my own destiny with great passion and abundant joie-de-vivre!

The wind is very strong today; full-bodied and powerful and alive. Like me, it too seems to be unleashed. It blows and bends the palms and coconut trees in wild, gay abandon; just for the sheer delight, playfulness and freedom of it all. It is the early afternoon and the sun is beaming brightly just overhead. And with the sun, the warmth, the visual sight and sound of the ocean, all seems right and bright and well with my world. And yet, that is not the full and complete story: it was not always right and bright and well. I relax, breathe, settle into my chair a little more comfortably, stare out into the ocean and remember... and remember...

I remember how my life was before all the unleashed discoveries; before the re-discoveries, the unleashed Fire, the unleashed Energy, the unleashed Passion and the unleashed Potential.

I was born and grew up on the island of Trinidad, in the Caribbean. The ocean and the sea and the waves and the beach held no appeal to me. I was rather sickly as a child. I suffered a lot from chest ailments with my lungs; asthma and bronchitis, which seemed always to lead to pneumonia. As such, getting wet and playing and splashing in the water and the ocean were never much of an option for me. I seemed to be always sick. I was told I was a 'cracked dish', for it seemed that whenever I got wet, I would 'catch' a cold. My chest had to be forever covered and wrapped up with a vest, no matter what the temperature. I was sure, as a child, that this 'encasement' stunted my development and my ability to grow breasts.

I remember, as a young girl, speaking with a stammer. I stuttered at times when trying to speak and get the words out. I was told by a doctor that I had a 'lazy tongue' and that I slurred my words. I couldn't seem to speak clearly or distinctly. I vaguely remember some discussion about me having an operation that could, would or should overcome and cure my speech impediment. The operation thankfully never took place.

The nosebleeds started not long after. I can't seem to recall at what age; 12 or 13 perhaps. I would bleed only from my right nostril. I seem to recall a lot of bleeding and blood… teacups full, in fact… as in, I'm sitting with a teacup perched under my right nostril and watching it fill up to the brim with blood! It was "…a true wonder and puzzlement where all the blood seemed to be coming from…" I was told. How idiotic and silly a statement! The conversations and discussions went on around me as if I were invisible and not even there. I guess in a way I wasn't. I started to remove mySelf from me and from the pain and chaos that seemed forever swirling around.

UNLEASHED!

I was taken back again to the doctors because by this time, I was also weak and insipid and feeling faint all the time. I needed more iron; I was anemic, I was told. Yet no amount of operations on my nostrils to cauterize the spots where the blood seemed to be gushing from, seemed to help. I would pop and burst another blood vessel somewhere else. My education and school-life suffered. I was told I was dense and stupid and a slow learner by my teachers. "It will be a wonder if she makes it out of high school", one teacher had remarked to my mother.

I was skinny as a rake, tall and lanky, boob-less, sickly, a 'cracked-dish' with no brains. What a combination! No one seemed to like me. I didn't seem to like me much either. The solution? Ship me off and send me abroad. Send me abroad to be educated. Perhaps a change of climate would help. It seemed to be the done thing in those days. Families in the Caribbean, who could afford it, sent their children abroad to be educated. It seemed to be rather a prestigious thing to do. I was told that it was a great privilege to be educated abroad.

My parents couldn't really afford to send me abroad, so they scrimped and saved in order to do so. My father had never had much of an education. He had never gone to high school. His family was large and very poor and for him, it was important to get out and earn a living. Yet, my father had a great love of music and in the early 1940's, he had joined an orchestra and learned to play the trumpet. Dad had met my mother while at the orchestra where she had played the violin.

I had always idolized the way my parents met and how romantic it had all seemed. In fact, they too had their own challenges of making their marriage relationship work. They were from different backgrounds. My father came from a very poor country family; my mother was raised in the city and was well educated. She had traveled abroad not long after World War II, completing her degree in Childhood Education and graduating from the University of Toronto in 1949. My parents were also from different religious backgrounds; my father was raised as a staunch Roman Catholic and my mother as an

Anglican. The difference between the Catholic and Anglican religions really seemed to matter in those days. They could not get married in the Catholic Church and my mother was not allowed to partake in the Communion of the Catholic Church. She had to sit in the back pew of the church at all times.

I pause and draw a breath. I find myself rambling along with stories that are no longer meaningful to me.

I was the keeper of a lot of the family secrets, as my mother before me had been. What I do remember is that as much as I would try to romanticize and idealize my childhood days, the truth as I know it and remember it in my belly and in my heart-of-hearts, was that my household as a child was one of a lot of turmoil and rage. The truth of the matter was that Dad was not just sleeping on the couch after dinner – he was in a drunken stupor. It was his way, I guess, of dealing and coping with problems - and there seemed to be lots of problems.

Problems with money and mortgage payments, as my mother tried to keep the family afloat and my Dad had no particular job. His grammatical English was poor (he didn't have much schooling and English was not his first language). I remember my mother always seemed to be correcting his speech. He resented this correction at times.

Then there was an occasion at night when he was tucking me into bed; when I knew that the goodnight kiss and hug and touch were different. I also kept that secret.

There was also a lot of anger with my brother growing up. He rebelled against the rules and any authority figure. There were beatings and punishment from my Dad in an effort to quell my brother's 'rebellious nature'. My mother had studied child psychology at University and did not believe in any form of corporal punishment. Her form of discipline was isolation and leaving me alone to get a 'grip on myself' and to behave in a 'right and proper manner'.

UNLEASHED!

Mum had left the home when I was two years old, as she had won a special scholarship that awarded her the opportunity to study in England, U.K. at the Institute of Child Studies. I had to be Mummy's big girl and to look after things. I had lots of make-believe friends and lived for many years in a fantasy world. In this world, I learned to talk about myself as 'Noreen'; as if I had been a fly on the wall looking in at my life and at myself. I was an observer of my life, as I simply stood passively and helplessly by and waited for it to unfold. I could do nothing... it was all too confusing and beyond me. All I wanted was to be the good girl, never rebellious, never naughty, always nice, always trying to please. I was the peacemaker, the one you could talk to, confide in, the reliable one, the trustworthy one. Good old dependable Noreen.

And yet I was always very sickly as a child. I have now come to realize that there was great intelligence in my being ill most of the time. My physical ailments kept people away from me. I was able to ward off unwanted attention. I was able to stop having to be the reliable and dependable one, at times.

My parents were apparently at their wits end with me. I was sent abroad to Canada to complete my Grade 12 and Grade 13 education. At first, it felt good to get away but when reality set in, I felt lost and alone and abandoned and betrayed. The allergies and the constant colds seemed to clear up somewhat but the nosebleeds continued. Well, at least two out of three wasn't so bad was it? My body didn't seem to think so and raged on all the more. I broke out in a rare form of measles, which no one else seemed to have had before, or since I'm sure. I could go on and on. As I have stated before, these physical manifestations of ailments I created, were very intelligent responses to what I was experiencing at the time, in my physical environment.

In an effort to supplement the cost of board and lodging while in Canada, I lived with the son and daughter-in-law of a girlfriend my mother had known while she had studied in Toronto in the 1950's. They had three kids who resented the heck out of me, the outsider. I had paid the family a monthly amount for my food and general upkeep; they were glad of the additional income. Matters quickly deteriorated when the wife requested that I lend her some money. Foolishly, I lent her the money that was allocated to pay my high school fees, as I was a foreign student. She never repaid the amount borrowed. When I couldn't pay the fees, the school threatened to have me deported. Needless to say, things got ugly. My mother was called and miraculously came up with additional funds to rectify matters.

I moved on - to other families, to complete my high school education and to everyone's surprise, including my own, I was accepted at the University of Toronto (my mother's old alma mater). I lived with a family then too, as it was cheaper than paying to live on campus at the university residence. With this particular family, I became the general maid, fact totem and baby sitter.

And yet to me, even with all the shifting around, matters didn't seem to improve much. At times it felt more like 'out of the frying pan into the fire'. It was amazing to me then what sordid and ugly secrets all families have. And I was the great keeper of the family secrets, even when it came to my own sexual assault at the hands of one of the family members who was considered by all to be so trusting and so good. After all, he was an honored war hero.

But that was then and this is now. I remember that I am 'in the now'... now in the year 2006, some 33 years later since I had first left Trinidad in 1973 when I was 16 years old. Until only recently I have, for the most part, been able to metabolize and process those feelings of extreme terror and rage and helplessness and betrayal. Emotions, which used to stop me dead in my tracks at the slightest trigger of some hidden recollection: a recollection that was very much outside my conscious awareness. Emotions, which had hampered me all my life in terms of attracting and creating relationships in which I truly felt any sense of trust. I become the Warrior Queen who always seemed to have to be on my guard in order to protect and defend. The emotions, stopped me 'cold' when it came to me mindfully choosing and engaging with boyfriends in any sort of loving relationship. I felt numb from the neck down and held myself leashed, reigned-in, withdrawn and 'in check' when it came to any form of intimacy.

As time progressed, my way of coping with all my internal chaos was to study and to keep busy. After much difficulty, I completed my four-year B.A. degree from the University of Toronto with a major in Economics. I remember now that I consciously took courses that were as far removed as possible from child education or child psychology or any field that my mother had previously taken or specialized in.

I returned to Trinidad and refused the help of my parents to connect me with people they knew who could help me get a job. I wanted to do this all on my own. I found out the hard way that it was not a matter of what you knew but whom you knew, when it came to easily getting a job on the island. Nevertheless I persevered and found a job at Barclays Bank as a Management Trainee. A few years later, I left Trinidad again for England and took courses at the Institute of Bankers. I then left for Scotland and graduated with an M.B.A. degree from the University of Stirling, specializing in Banking and Finance. I returned to Trinidad and was there for a number of years before I came back to Canada again, now as a landed immigrant. I applied and obtained my Canadian citizenship a few years later.

Over the years, as was now my habit or pattern, I continued to study. It was as if I had to constantly prove to myself, over and over again, that the teachers who had said I was dumb and stupid were wrong. And yet no amount of studying, people congratulating me and telling me other wise, or me staring at the certificates I dutifully framed and hung up on my walls, seemed to eradicate my feelings of being dumb. Those feelings of inadequacy seemed to be indelibly and forever etched and wired into my brain.

I continued on in the financial field and completed the Mutual Funds course of study and the Canadian Securities course. Next, I received my Certified Investment Manager's designation (CIM) and the Certified Financial Planner's designation (CFP). I took a Securities Options course and later studied to obtain my Fellowship at the Canadian Securities Institute – an FCSI designation and certificate. Two years of study after that, I completed Level I and Level II in the Insurance field in order to obtain my Life Insurance License. And a year or so later, I was off studying again in order to receive my Elder Planning Counselor's (EPC) designation. In addition to all this formal studying with its various designations, for the past five years I have been taking other mandatory forms of courses and programs in order to meet the 30 hours of continuing educational (C.E.) credits stipulated for the financial field that I am in. And my search for 'more' - and a more meaningful existence - continued unabated.

I noticed that I enjoyed working in the financial field and having direct contact with the people who were becoming my customers and clients. I got to be very passionate when speaking with my clients about their investments and their need to make informed choices about their money. A long time before, my own parents had suffered a great loss financially when they had invested $120,000 from my mother's severance/pension package as a retired school inspector, into a private company and lost every penny. Needless to say, this had also caused further emotional hardship and discord in our family relationship.

I noticed when dealing with many of my clients, whether they were financially stable and well-off or not, that they too appeared to be searching for 'more'. No matter how much they traveled on holiday, delved into their favorite hobbies or leisure activities, spent time with their families, kept up a frantic pace of being busy at all times (being on committees, various boards, volunteer work, joining clubs or societies), there still seemed to be an unquenchable thirst for meaningfulness. Not that any of this busy-ness was good/bad, right or wrong, I just began to pay attention and to notice: to observe and notice this restlessness in others and more importantly, to notice this restlessness in myself.

I noticed especially in my female clients that in a number of cases, they seemed to have persistent feelings of depression, sadness, great loneliness even with having a spouse or partner and/or children and grandchildren. In some cases, others revealed to me feelings of anxiety, uncontrollable rage, great anger, betrayal and at times feelings of suicide. I could well relate to those feelings, as I too had experienced those emotions as well, at one time or another in my own life. I felt compelled to do something, but what could I do? I was only their financial advisor and furthermore, what business of mine was it anyway?

I came up with the idea of running a series of seminars for women, by women. In early 2002, I held a series of five seminars to educate and motivate women and their daughters. The overall theme of the seminars was under the banner of 'things every woman should know and be aware of'. My guest speakers were a female accountant, a female lawyer, an insurance specialist, myself speaking on financial matters and finally, I had a motivational speaker in the form of Louise LeBrun from the WEL-Systems® Institute. After all, I passionately believed in individuals making informed choices; for me it was not a question of "just trust me" and "sign on the dotted line". I was not sure where all this education was leading, but felt sure that it would help somehow.

I reflect as I write this, that I was very much in a 'protection' mode of thinking, as opposed to that of 'growth and expansion'. After all, I reasoned, the world was not a safe and abundant place. I felt, as I had for the past 40-odd years, that I had to protect and defend myself and the interests of my clients. They had to know and be made aware of the many dangers and pitfalls when it came to money and investing. 'Motivation by fear', as I have now come to call it: notions and ideas for leaving one feeling, small and vulnerable and helpless and puny.

It was in connecting with Louise and the WEL-Systems Institute and taking a number of their programs over the past four years, that I began to wake up and become fully alive. This feeling of being in alignment with mySelf... of being fully present and alive is very different for me. In my area of expertise as a Financial Consultant, I had taken numerous motivational courses and programs. Courses on how to be at your 'peak performance'; courses on how to 'amaze clients' and create for them 'ultimate experiences'; courses on how to 'stay pumped and motivated' - and I could go on and on. Yet for all of these courses and programs while putting me on a 'high' in the moment, the 'thrill of the message' - like my numerous certificates and designations - would quickly fizzle and fade with time.

How the heck was I to remain 'upbeat and pumped' when it came to my own life, far less for trying to motivate and stimulate someone else's? And more importantly to me, as I was to discover, was the question of why could I not stay upbeat and pumped? I thought I was making the right choices. I had spent a lot of money on courses to keep me 'on track'. I had paid keen attention in the classes and taken copious notes to revise and remember. What was holding me back? Why this constant 'restlessness' within mySelf? Who was I or 'mySelf' anyway? Who was I becoming?

The first course I took from the WEL-Systems Institute was *Igniting the Self* in the late summer of 2002. I began to awaken; to become truly aware of and rediscover and embrace my ability to be creative. I began to literally feel the awakening in the very fiber of my body and not just by saying it over and over to myself, as I had in previous motivational courses in the hope that something would 'stick'. All I had to do was simply to breathe; to begin to pay attention to the many times I would catch or hold on to my breath and stop the flow of emotion (or what I later learned to think of as 'energy') from moving in my body, whenever I felt criticized or I didn't follow the 'rules'. I gave myself permission to 'know the truth' of my own experience and to stop being dishonest with myself as things 'happened to me'. I write 'happened to me' in quotation marks, as this way of thinking was also to change for me, as I reclaimed my life: I may have been victimized and traumatized by happenings in my past, but I certainly was no longer a victim!

I waited two more years until October 2004 before I embarked on the second program at the Institute called **Resourcefulness in Action**. I'm not quite sure why I waited so long. I think perhaps I was partly afraid of the unabashed questions that I was constantly asking myself. I found myself questioning and challenging many things that I had previously held as 'sacred and true' for me. Things about which, when I told myself the truth, I didn't like the answers I was coming up with. And more astounding and unsettling for me were the things I had <u>no answers</u> for!

Quite a revelation for me: all my training and ways of thinking, I had prided myself in being very cold, analytical and rational in order to provide answers and solutions for myself and my clients. My thinking head could not come up with any answers at all to my new questions. As I was to later discover and to joyfully accept, declare and embrace, "…my confusion was and is a gateway or portal into my own continuous growth and evolution". I don't have to have all the answers or, for that matter, any answers and that is just fine with me.

I learned 'to stay in the tough conversations' with myself, my family, my boyfriend at the time and my clients. I learned to stick with what was true and meaningful to me, without being constantly afraid that I was going to offend someone or without constantly trying to please everyone. No, I was no longer going to visit Aunt Sibyl anymore and here was why. No, I wasn't content to stay in bed all Sunday mornings and 'make love' as I had done in the past and here was why. No, I did not have any 'hot stock picks' for your portfolio like before and here was why.

Then lo and behold, I re-discovered that I could say 'no' without any explanation whatsoever, if I so chose! I gave myself permission to simply change my mind. Wow! Powerful stuff for me and yet so freeing and liberating in my body! And yes - most definitely - there were consequences and repercussions to be had when I had dared to step outside the 'norm' and to challenge the rules. However, I also learned that the cost of simply going blindly along and following along or mindlessly repeating what I'd previously done or what my cultural conditioning had said I should do, was taking a tremendous, detrimental toll on my body.

This life, it is said "...is not a dress rehearsal." This is it! Therefore, for me to do nothing but passively observe the world as it merrily trots on by, was not any longer an option that I was contented with. And my body applauded my willingness to engage my life differently! The nosebleeds that had haunted me for years stopped and eventually disappeared. The severe cramps, pain and heavy flow I would have during my period that used to have me well medicated for a few days, again mysteriously disappeared. My migraine headaches started to ease and become less frequent. As I breathed and relaxed into my body, I would get great insights and brilliant thoughts on how I could change, create, transform and do things differently for myself and my clients. And I was discovering that I can have great fun along the way. I did not have to do serious things, seriously.

The momentum of my discoveries about mySelf in the Fall of 2004, had me eagerly registering and looking forward to the next experience in the series, entitled *Influencing with Intention: Mastering Self Creation* which was to commence at the end of July 2005. The theme of this program was "Be Willing to Stand Alone".

On the morning of June 7th, 2005 my mother in Trinidad had a fall and died: she was 87 years old. The bottom felt as if it had fallen out of my world. Everything shifted and would never be the same again. I was now literally 'standing alone' and did not want to be. My relationship with my parents and my mother especially, had been somewhat strained, to say the least, when I was growing up. I had blamed my mother for a lot of stuff and had held myself cut off from her, in more ways than one, from the time I first left home at the age of 16. Over the years, I had accepted the role of the dutiful daughter and had wanted to please both my parents. My father had died on Christmas Eve in 1999. He had had a long battle with the Alzheimer's disease and had mercifully died from other complications.

As I had begun to rediscover myself and who I was capable of becoming, with the courses and programs at the WEL-Systems Institute, I began to re-connect with my mother in very meaningful and engaging ways for me. I had the courage to de-cloak to her my feelings of inadequacy and rage; and the experience of the sexual assault. No longer did I want to keep my feelings hidden. We had the opportunity to air and openly discuss the so-called 'family secrets'. My de-cloaking seemed to give her permission to also tell me of her own experiences and the family secrets of her own past.

The cycle of passively engaging life and merely 'going along to get along'; of keeping the secrets and always being stoic, was finally broken for us. I could say to her out loud, "I love you Maman", "I am so very proud of you, Maman". With my mother's death, I felt that I had lost my great friend and confidante. I was angry with myself that I didn't have more time to spend with her and to really get to know this 'genius' of a woman. And yet, in life, I firmly believe that everything is unfolding as it should: our time together was just 'right', and will always be treasured.

Even though I initially thought of rescheduling the course, as I intellectually didn't feel ready with all the upheaval that was going on in my life at the time, my body was very ready for more growth and more discoveries. I was restless. I hungered for more and was not willing to wait for the next program that would have taken place in the Fall. I engaged, and I am so thankful that I did.

In January 2006, I completed the final rigorous twelve-day program at the WEL-Systems Institute, called *Catalyst for Change*. By working on mySelf, I have become an invitation, an attraction, a contagion, an opportunity, a catalyst for those with whom I come in contact, to engage their lives differently as I have mindfully chosen to engage my own life, to the fullest.

Along the way of my perpetually unfolding self-discoveries, I have paid attention to the signposts and lessons which have meaningfully impacted the shift in perception of my life. As my perception has shifted, I have changed. More importantly the very cells in my body have re-ordered and rewired themselves with new and different ways of thinking. I have awakened to my own brilliance… to my own genius and my restlessness and thirst for growth and for more. I share with you but two of these signposts and lessons as follows: -

1) I am responsible for my own life and the direction that I wish it to take. I chart my own course and I set my own sail.
    As simple or as obvious as this notion or expression may seem, it was a real eye opener for me.
    For so many years (I would say at least for the past 30 years; I just turned 49 on February 20th), I truly believed that someone else, some circumstance outside of mySelf, was responsible for the way I was presently living my life and for the way my life was unfolding. Previously, for the most part, I mindlessly drifted through my life and never gave it much thought at all. I now hold mySelf 'at cause' rather than 'at effect'.

    I remember to breathe, to pause and to mindfully choose how I wish to respond to a given situation. Do I fly off the handle and get myself all worked up and worried, or do I remember who I am and who I have become? I notice that when I breathe/draw breath, remember to keep my body open and relaxed with my attention grounded at the base of my spine, I speak without a stutter - very forcefully, very powerfully with a clear intention and purpose for what I want. More importantly, I unequivocally ask for what I want with a very clear and precise intention and I discovered that I can manifest and shape my future.

2) I notice that in my business practice, I have redefined who I am as a Financial Consultant. I have also redefined who I am as a Human Being.

I am no longer a 'stock picker' when it comes to my clients' investments. I now create meaningful solutions to my select group of investors, to ensure that they have financial confidence and WEL-Being. For me, it is no longer just about the money. It is about Quality of Life; it is about being and staying awake and present to our lives as they unfold. It is about Dignity of Choice. It is about vitality and fun and playfulness and curiosity and connectivity with ourselves and with others.

I ask my clients' questions such as "What's important about money… to you? What's the most important thing about being A-L-I-V-E… to you?" And I stay in the tough conversations, even when my clients have never thought about, or had anyone ask them such questions: even when they have no replies to, or answers for, the questions. I see them pause and ponder and think anew. For as I have discovered for myself, our power is in the size and courage of our questions, not in the accuracy of our answers. My clients' reactions have been overwhelming. They say they enjoy our financial reviews more than ever and look forward to our discussions and conversations. They feel inspired and enlivened, and also want to go out and engage their lives differently.

I consider mySelf a 'work-in-progress'. I completely amaze myself when I "…come to the edge…" and engage my own life. Every time I make my choices by standing in the here and now, looking boldly into the future and creating the life that I want for myself, a change and a difference occurs. My world becomes so much more, by me just being my authentic self.

It is a great joy and a tremendous pleasure for me to discover again that I do indeed have the freedom to move, to mindfully choose: the freedom to express myself, with gay abandon and to know, absolutely, that I am creating my life and my future, on my own terms. This permission and freedom that I re-discovered in myself is a great gift that we all can and **must give to ourselves**. It is a gift for me that is very precious and divine. It is a gift that has allowed me to continue to want to grow and to build and to create and to thrive and to bloom and to flourish exceedingly, and to be all that I can possibly be!

Noreen Mejias believes that you can live a rich and meaningful life! She has the ability to bring her passion for life and an impressive track record together in helping you to do just that. She is both willing and able to work with you to strengthen and protect your resources as a gateway to expansive living.

Noreen has been in the financial services industry since 1986, providing specialized investment planning services since 1996. With impressive credentials, well-honed skills and the wisdom that comes with experience, she is an accomplished investment professional. Noreen brings comprehensive financial planning services and a variety of financial products to her clients – and much more.

UNLEASHED!

The Journey Home

Jackie Zirpdji

To consider myself magnificent despite the mistakes, the questions, the outbreaks, the disappointments, the confusion, the self-doubt is truly the most significant change that I have accomplished over the past five years. To engage them seriously as I would have done in the past, will only slow me down and take my energy away from what it is that I want to create with my life. And so it is with great excitement that I share with you my story as an invitation to discover and trust your own magnificence.

I marvel at how ordinary my story actually is. No physical abuse, no drugs or alcoholism, no divorce or major conflicts, no burnout or depression, just a story of an immigrant family led by loving parents looking for a life with more opportunities for their four daughters. And within this seemingly ordinary story, I developed beliefs about myself and my world that had me making choices that kept me small for many years.

When I think back to my childhood, there is very little content that I can share with you. I can tell you that I was born in Egypt, the youngest of four girls. My parents were also born in Egypt and are of Armenian and Greek descent. Many will be inspired by this rich cultural heritage and intellectually, I would agree with them. Emotionally, I have often felt anywhere from embarrassed to frustrated to angry that, in fact, so little of this richness was ever considered as important enough to keep alive through our shared stories and traditions. There were more practical things to do and to think about. We left/escaped from Egypt when I was five years old and the conversations and intention to do so had started long before that. My experience of Egypt is truly a great metaphor for my life. With no conscious memories, less than a handful of pictures, no conversations, there is nothing that can reflect back to me those first five years of my life; a sense of Self, a sense of who I was.

My parents' need to be practical became even more important when they immigrated to Canada with their four daughters, both of them 40 years of age and with little money. The emphasis continued to be our safety and security. I believe, although I do not recollect, that even as a young child I knew that there must be more important things to do and talk about; there must be different ways of being.

This experience was coupled with the experience of being or at least of acting differently from my sisters and having attributes that had me labeled as 'garcon manqué' (tomboy), the literal definition is 'missed boy'. With much attention and emphasis placed on being well-behaved, quiet and well-groomed pretty little girls, there was little reinforcement or encouragement for me to be me. In fact, being me left me mostly alone and very angry. I had little to hang on to that confirmed that who I was, was magnificent. And so began my adult life. The anger had by then turned into sadness.

The first ten years of my adult life revolved around relationships, around being loved. Little did I know that the invitation that was being given to me was to love myself. The other important aspects of my life had been well taken care of – the education and the well-paid job in my field of economics had been secured. But with no clear sense of who I was (having had it denied for many years), I had relationships with passionate individuals who had a great sense of what they wanted - and what they wanted became what I wanted. It wasn't all bad. Other people's passions held great benefits for me. I learned to ski; I ran a marathon; I learned to play blackjack; I learned how to make a mean curry; I campaigned in municipal elections. But I didn't have anything to give back – just myself.

As I look back, I realize that so many of my choices continued the pattern of leaving me alone; sometimes angry, more often sad and in despair. I was given so many opportunities to become comfortable with my solitude, opportunities to reclaim who I was, but I would require more invitations before I was ready to do so. From the outside looking in, many most-likely saw me as a successful, independent woman. I was both those things, financially speaking, but I remained dependent on other people to define me. I, by myself, had never been good enough.

It is only recently that I realized how I rebelled against the practical nature of many of my parents' attitudes about work, about money, about housecleaning, about friends and extended family, about school, about what to talk about around the dinner table, about almost everything. The depth of life - much like the richness of our heritage - had to be considered, explored, and talked about. It couldn't be all about good jobs, clean houses and what other people thought. By the time I was in my early 30's, I was searching for more. I was beginning to re-connect with that part of my Self that wanted to contribute more. My job at Bell Canada was leaving me less than fulfilled, with all my efforts making little apparent difference in the world. So whether I began adopting a 'not like my parents' strategy or whether I was beginning to connect with Self or a combination of both, the search had begun. I was restless. I did not want to settle.

Interestingly enough, the first stop on the search was Church. I began to feel deeply connected with the Christian community, a journey that would evolve over a period of ten years. Many of my choices in that period of time were influenced by a desire and commitment to be 'the hands and feet of Jesus'. It is this message that inspired me to take a leave from Bell Canada and pursue studies that would be more aligned with making a contribution, although what contribution I wanted to make was not clear.

In this search, I discovered the area of Wellness and began to be very interested in the holistic approach associated with that field. I completed a year of studies in Wellness and had plans to return to Bell to see what I could do to support people in achieving an improved quality of life. While I was pursuing these 'professional' interests, concurrently, on the personal scene, I had met and was engaged to marry the director of a food bank in Montreal, Martin, a gentleman who was also studying to be an Anglican minister. It was all starting to make sense. I felt a deep sense of belonging; a deep sense of purpose, a deep sense that I was being 'the hands and feet of Jesus' and then, it all fell apart... or so I thought.

After two years, my engagement ended after months of what was defined to me as a 'time-out' by Martin. I was told that the time-out was needed because of my anger problem. Although I felt connected to Martin because of what I believed to be a shared purpose, I continued to feel like the invisible partner. Again, most of the time we were doing what was important to him and this time I engaged this feeling of invisibility with anger rather than sadness. We were never alone because even when we were alone he always had at least one book with him. He would read it - in restaurants, at the dinner table, in bed - as if I weren't even there; much like my sisters when I just wanted someone to play with.

We went to Florida and spent much of our time visiting churches and Christian bookstores. If I wanted to be on the beach, I needed to do it alone. And despite my many requests to be seen, things did not change. So, I did anger the only way I knew how, the way I had always done it in my family: loud and with a lot of intensity, the only way I believed I could be seen and heard. Over and above all, and interestingly enough, within the context of a more meaningful life built on Christian values and helping others, there were many practical issues that emerged, like money and housework and dinner and I was doing it all. I am glad that I recognized that my `not like my parents` strategy might not always be useful. And I did more anger. The Fire was moving in ways that were not serving me because I was still there taking it all. I was continuing to define myself through others but now, I was not accepting it very graciously.

On the professional scene, I had come back from my wellness studies with intentions of creating a Wellness program in Bell, only to be met with an accounting classification job. The organization was not ready to consider such a program and with downsizing, that was the only job that was available. After two years of searching for more meaningful work, my efforts were being shunned.

I moved through a long period of confusion and despair, not believing that I was what appeared to be, back at square one. For the first time, everything that was important had been present. Most importantly, this had been a call from God. How could it go wrong?

I moved through that difficult time turning to prayer, and the support of my minister and my friends, including Daniel.

I had never felt a sense of connection beyond myself as deeply as I sensed Jesus' presence when the Fire moved through me, although I did not know what that meant at the time. In that moment, and with great ease, things shifted for me more quickly than I had ever experienced. I was going to start thinking of myself. I wanted a family. I wanted to be loved and accepted. I broke off the time-out with Martin to start dating my now-husband of almost 12 years, Daniel, who had been on the sidelines for a few months waiting with his invitation of love. I was 36 years old. Within a year, I had a job transfer to Ottawa in an economics function, Daniel and I were married, we had moved to Chelsea, we were building a house and we were expecting our first child.

The four years that followed were exciting. We were building a family and now had two daughters, Alexandra and Alyson. Daniel was at home with the girls. At work, I had successfully created a wellness program and was doing very well in a new HR position. Then the invitation to move on came again. With changes in management, the wellness program was not going to receive the same resources that it had. My choices: return to an Economics function or leave. I had tasted what it was like to make a personally significant contribution. I could not go back and the only way forward seemed to be to leave a 20-year career at Bell Canada. I chose to leave; I could not settle. That choice put me on a new course. The search was on again and this time the stop on the search was The WEL-Systems Institute (then, Partners in Renewal).

With a coaching business as my new professional endeavour and as an extension of the contribution that I had made with the wellness program at Bell, I engaged the first Institute program, looking forward to developing the skills that would make me a successful coach. What I discovered was a great opportunity to learn more about myself, the strategies that I was using in my relationships and in my life. What I also learned was a new way of experiencing myself. And then it happened: another turning point in my life, a knowing deep in my body. With my attention in my body, I connected energetically with an immense sense of wanting to contribute – I remember myself saying, "there is so much that I want to do" And for the first time in what was going to be many, many times, Louise LeBrun supported me in breathing through the feelings that accompanied that thought, as I wept. That connection with my Self was when I first knew that there was no turning back.

So who was I in that moment in time? Despite the new awareness, there remained many struggles, much confusion and self-doubt. Books had been the enemy; I believed that I was not well read. I didn't know enough; my vocabulary was limited; I could not speak eloquently. I couldn't manage alone; I was not resourceful enough. I was a mother. I was scared to compromise any time with my children. I wanted to see them grow, be there for them. I was serious and I continued to be angry. I loved my children more than anything in the world and still there were many times that my response was to shout and even to spank. And I knew without a doubt in my mind, being motivated with this immense sense of wanting to contribute that I needed to continue to grow. I could start tasting the possibilities of making a difference and there were too many obstacles standing in the way. I could not see my strengths; I could not see my magnificence. I could only sense the pull of the call. I followed. But before I could change the world, I had to change from within. Although my life on the surface was good, inside there were too many questions, it just wasn't good enough, I could not settle.

And what an invitation I had from my Self, and from my children to do so. My children became my guide. I became curious about my responses to them having learned that through those responses I could learn more about myself. I became acutely aware of my influence on their sense of Self, on their capacity to speak and create, on their courage to dream. I began to pay great attention to the space that I was giving them, the space to choose for themselves, to speak for themselves and to be themselves. I wanted to model through my actions and my choices, through my conversations and my questions, through my emotions and my vulnerabilities what I wanted for them. They became as much a catalyst for my desire to grow, as did the call from my Self.

At the same time, I had the full support of Daniel to continue this journey. He and I created the space for each other to explore and become, and at first I experienced his unique way of engaging life as frustrating and later as refreshing. It was through trusting him that I began to see that indeed the beliefs, values and attitudes that I held as right may not be so. After all, I had screwed up at least as often as him was how I reasoned it back then. So I started relaxing into considering another way of being. He was great prep work for the work I was about to do with the WEL-Systems Institute.

As all of this was happening, so was life. There were money issues: we started making expensive choices about child-care and school, Daniel wasn't working yet and I was still getting the business off the ground. There were family issues, with my sisters not visiting us very often. My parents weren't quite sure about our choices and were letting us know about it. We were allowing ourselves to feel manipulated by Daniel's father and the promise of financial gifts. Our best friend Judy died.

Looking back at it, I believe that I moved through those times in ways that I would not have been able to without that connection with Self, without a greater awareness that I now had about who I was.

The following year I completed the WEL-Systems programs and was now a WEL-Systems Catalyst. I felt so connected to the community and especially to Louise and Gwen. I had spent hundreds of hours with them in programs as they created opportunities for movement and hopefulness. I felt accepted and encouraged in a way that I had only felt with Daniel before. By the time I had completed the programs, I had moved through many of the beliefs about myself that had been keeping me stuck.

I began to know that I had been invisible to myself, to my strengths and my accomplishments. I began to understand (although not to the extent that I do today) that my ability to be with people far outweighed the knowledge that I had to share with them. I became aware that my biggest fear was to be alone and curious as to how I had created that situation for myself many times in my life. I became even more aware of my intention: I wanted to change those systems that influenced children's lives, now, more than ever aware of the extent of our role as adults in their beliefs about themselves and their world.

It was all starting to make sense again. I felt a deep sense of belonging; a deep sense of purpose, a deep sense that I was part of the WEL-Systems community. I had setup shop at the WEL-Systems Institute (WSI) and was sharing an office with fellow Catalysts, Susan and Greg. I was creating my business, wanting to coach and run WEL-Systems programs. And then the unexpected happened: I had a fallout with Louise. In response to a request, I created a bio for a speaking engagement that I was doing on behalf of the WSI. The comments that I received from Gwen and Louise were that I was showing up in my bio more as mother than I was as WEL-Systems Associate. I experienced the comments as a denial of who I was, much like my early experiences of family. How could Gwen and Louise, after they had supported me in finding Self deny the Self that I was showing them? I responded with intense rage that carried with it the experience of all the moments in my life that others had not acknowledged who I was. I was devastated. I felt angry, I felt guilty, I felt embarrassed. The connection had been broken. I couldn't believe that the search was on again. This time the stop on the search was going to be my Self.

I moved through the next few months continuing to be deeply committed to sharing with others what I myself had learned through the WSI programs. I was creating my future and I was going to move through this experience with curiosity and intention. I found in myself the courage and creativity to develop a two-day program *The Essence of You*. The intention of the program was to create an experience which would lead people to understanding themselves better, be exposed to the WEL-Systems models, have conversations and movement of energy that would re-connect them with their Self. Any wonder that that would be what I would want to give others?

The next turning point in my journey was the first two times that I delivered *The Essence of You*. What incredible results! I discovered that I was able to hold the space for people to make huge discoveries not because of what I knew but simply because of my presence. I had done it alone. I was energized and exuberant.

Many of the participants wanted to stay connected and became personal coaching clients and the results were astounding. My clients were starting to see choices that they had never believed available to them. And then they started making choices that changed their lives – new jobs, new relationships, a new sense of Self, shifts in how they expressed themselves, with their children, with their partners… it went on and on, evidence and encouragement that I was on the right path. The ease with which I worked with The CODE Model™ and the eagerness with which my clients engaged it encouraged me to keep going. I had finally come home to my Self. I was doing what I loved to do and I was doing it well simply by being me. What a feeling!

The initial high did not come without future self-doubt. Over the three-year period that brings us to the summer of 2005 (6 months ago) I experienced average success at creating as many programs and attracting as many clients as I wanted. When I was working things were great but I wasn't working enough. Thankfully, other contracts were coming in to help with cash flow but were taking me away from the work that I wanted. On the home front Daniel had started his own business and the time and energy that he had been giving to the family affairs shifted. I found myself taking care of family progressively more and with whatever time was left, taking care of business. And my anger and resentment signaled to me that I needed to make a choice.

I had finally found my Self and knew what I wanted my contribution to be – to help others do what I had taken so painstakingly long to do: find Self. If I was going to have the impact that I wanted to have, I needed to give it my energy. Or, I could continue doing what I was doing. I wanted to make a conscious choice rather than allow circumstances make it for me. I chose to give all I had to my business and I knew, without a doubt, that I wanted it to be a WEL-Systems based business. It was time to re-connect with the WEL-Systems Institute and now that I knew I could do it alone, it was time to come back to the community that shared my intention because I wanted to do it with others.

And so who am I now? Let me share with you a few recent conversations that I have had with myself and with my family that reflect my current reality:

As I was driving Alexandra to school one morning, I was sharing with her how much my finger hurt and how I thought that it may be broken, something I had exclaimed to her several times the day before when I injured it. So she said, "Well, mom, why don't you do something about it?". "Because I don't want to be sitting in a hospital waiting room for 3 hours", I replied. "Well, would you be doing it if I had broken my finger?" "Of course", I said to which she replied, "that doesn't make sense". And I heard myself saying, "I know but somehow you are more important than me". She said, "MOM! That doesn't make sense" and I said, "I know, but that is how I am living my life" and I cried the rest of the way to my destination.

And I wonder, is that the next step on the road to Self

I continue to stay awake to it all............

In my family we have come full circle. My parents have been living with us for 1.5 years now and I know that they have noticed that Daniel and I make different parenting choices than the ones that they did when their children were young. Curiously enough, they commend us for those choices, the same choices that they had once questioned, mostly out of fear and love. They congratulate us for being great parents and are proud of their granddaughters.

I came home one evening. Alyson had been alone with her grandparents and my mother had as she described it "told Alyson something about her behavior so that she would know how to behave when she was out with others". And my father told her "stop telling the girls what to do, that's why Jackie lets them do whatever they want because you didn't let her be" – and my mother asked is that true – "did you tell him that". And the reality was that I hadn't. Has my father noticed a 'not like my mother strategy'? Do I really let them do whatever they want to do? Is that OK – for them, for me? Is it time for me to question my choices?

I continue to stay awake to it all............

I notice that I walk around angry most of the time, or do I? Has it become easier for me to notice the energy signature associated with anger more so than the one associated with joy and contentment? Is angry the only way that I recognize myself as being? And how I fear it for Alyson.

Do I have the right to be writing a chapter in the Sekhmet Rising book with such a fundamental question still lurking after all this time?

And then I notice that I get angry when I haven't been able to please, to make things right for people (even something as simple as "Mom, I don't have any clean underwear."). And so no wonder - how can I make things right for everyone - what an impossible request of myself. Is it time for me to question my choices?

I continue to stay awake to it all............

For months now, I have been driving by this new building in my community. Every time I do so, I visualize a Women's Wellness Center, an intention that I hold as part of my unfolding. And when Gwen asks me what has kept me from engaging those thoughts, I notice that I hold that intention as too extraordinary for me. And then I find out that the building has been leased. And I wonder how many other ideas that I have held as extraordinary feats I have allowed to slip by, caught in the turmoil of my thoughts about what is possible for me, of who I am capable of becoming, having grown up in a world where being extraordinary was not something that was even contemplated. And I am ready to move beyond the context that was defined to me for what is possible.

I continue to stay awake to it all............

And I am reminded to breathe, follow the impulse and allow myself to know my truth….

As you can see through these stories, 'issues' have not disappeared. As I continue to be in relationship with my children and my husband, my sisters and my parents, my colleagues and my friends, with my self and my business, life continues to unfold: the outbreaks, the confusion, the self-doubt, the money issues, the housework issues, the school issues. What I notice though is how differently I move through them – awake, and therefore with a greater sense of trust and confidence and courage.

For now, it feels like I am riding those waves and moving through them with much greater ease. The difference for me is that I am now experiencing them in the context of my magnificent Self, with my attention on my intention, being who I am wherever I go and never alone. Now that I am no longer invisible to myself, I am no longer invisible to others. I take the space that I am wherever I go and things change. Some people fall away from my life and others feel the attraction to enter it and it's all OK.

And this is my story. It is paradoxical for me that I should be completing it this Easter weekend. I grew up in the Catholic tradition, although religion was practiced quite loosely. It is only in writing this story that I realized the extent to which religion played a role in my evolution.

As I have previously mentioned, there was a time where my own search for meaning in life had me consider the Christian religious traditions with a much greater sense of passion and commitment, finding great meaning in the rituals. My understanding of God has evolved considerably and in God and Jesus, I see much more clearly the invitation to be my Self, not to be his hands and feet but to be my own. When I celebrate Jesus now, I celebrate a person who was completely connected with Self. I believe that there in lies his divinity, to be completely true to his sense of purpose in this time and space. And there in lies the invitation to me that I now extend to you.

I have completed this chapter, a true reflection that I have come a long way. Writing a chapter in a book is something that I would never have dreamt of, even up to 6 months ago. But now, I am once again connected with my magnificent Self as I was in the moment of my conception and I allow the words to flow from that place as naturally as did the cry to be fed, and everything has become much easier.

Jackie Zirpdji, CODE Model Coach™, facilitator and educator is the founder of Transformations+, a WEL-Systems based business. Jackie is passionate about life and human potential and this makes her invitation to others to consider what is possible for them very authentic. She combines her talent for asking great questions with her talent for being present to the unfolding of the answers to create life-altering experiences for all those that she works with as coaching clients or program participants

The Journey Home

Finding My Magic... Within

Patricia Donihee

It is one of those late Canadian winter days. You know the ones, when you first begin to feel the warmth of the sun on your upturned face and you fill your lungs with the delicious smell of approaching spring. Oh, you know there will be another storm or two but the promise of spring's unfolding is present and you know it - just as I know I hold deep inside me the promise of unfolding messages as I hold the pen and make the marks on this page!

It feels like the message has been growing, developing and waiting to be born for years. It is probably more accurate to say that I stumbled around for years, attempting to express the incessant rumblings inside in a way that made sense. I became aware of my inner rumblings at a pretty young age but I had no idea what they were or what to do about them. What I was noticing and questioning was so different from what I heard from everyone else around me. Sometimes, I actually spoke my thoughts or questions out loud and was silenced by the censoring responses I received. Although my voice was silenced for a long, long time, the inner rumblings never went away and were never silenced - they only went underground.

This is a story of awakening - of my awakening - to the transformational power of my magic within. It is my story of the Fire that refused to be extinguished, even though it did get buried pretty deeply and with significant consequences to my health. It is my story of the magic within me, always seeking ways to express the genius within. And as I write these words,

I wonder: did Sekhmet ("she who is powerful") ever struggle to formulate her message? Speak her truth? When she was "removing threats and punishing those who do wrong against Ma'at," was she doing so as "healer, mother, and protector" or as "patron of Physician-Priests and Healers," roles often overshadowed by "the fact she is sometimes destructive?" "Sekhmet's action is always right or appropriate action. It is never chaotic or random. It is always what is needed at the time."[1]

What is needed in our world at this time? What is happening to us; to our daughters, granddaughters, our sisters and our friends? There are epidemics of what the medical model calls "depression; eating disorders; fibromyalgia and chronic fatigue; 'addictions' to substances, to things and to people." 'Happy drugs' are advertised like candy. Children are killing children and whole nations are dying in preventable epidemics. My belief is that what is needed is for women who have awakened to their magic within to share the story of their journey and become a beacon to guide other women!

This is the story of my awakening; the story of my lifelong commitment to curiosity, to being all it was possible for me to be, no holds barred, no matter what! Having finally awakened to my own magic within, I am determined to stay awake and to be an invitation to other women to discover their possibility inside. This is also a story of a journey from a vibrant, healthy, curious child to a chronically ill, discouraged and silent adult; to an awakened, vibrant, mature and wise crone who is now totally unwilling to be silenced!

Who would have ever guessed it? Me, living in my dream house overlooking the water, in a place I can only describe as magical. It is as peaceful as it is breathtakingly beautiful. Some days, I am in awe of the fact that my husband and I were able to co-create this wonderful place. We carved the spot for the house out of the side of a hill. The house is surrounded on three sides by woods, most of which we own. The fourth side

---

1   http://showcase.netins.net/web/ankh/sekhmet1.html

offers a 180-degree view of the Kennebecasis River. We have deer in our front yard and all kinds of songbirds on our deck. The night sky is so clear and bright, and overflowing with stars, you feel like you can reach out and just grab a handful! From our open bedroom window you can smell the water and hear the waves. You can watch the sailboats in summer and the snowflakes swirl and dance in the winter. You can hear the loon's call, watch seagulls soar and the crows torment the eagles. The sunrises are full of hope and the sunsets take your breath away with their promise of another day. The landscape, never the same, is uniquely beautiful and different everyday of the year, regardless of the weather. It is easy to marvel at the magnificence of the nature that surrounds us!

I get up every morning with passion in my heart and joy in my step as I walk down the stairs to my office to begin my day. Creating a private counselling, coaching and mediation practice, and my lifelong drive to be 'healer', became the invitation to my awakening, but I am getting ahead of myself.

Throughout this journey, it has helped that I have always loved learning; the smell of new notebooks, the excitement of an unread book, the buzz of the crowd at a workshop or conference. I am vaccinated with a travel map and I am endlessly curious about new places and people. I believe life is a joyous experience to be lived to the fullest and the best is yet to come! But for now, the beginning...

I was born in 1941 to a university-educated father and a well-educated mother, just prior to my father's Second World War military service. My Dad left when I was a year old and came back when I was almost 5. In later years, we came to realize how blessed we were as a family that my dad came home. My parents set about rebuilding their life and I soon became a big sister.

I had my appendix out when I was about 5½ and I also remember episodes where I would be doubled over with 'pain' in my belly that would take my breath away. The summer between grades 8 and 9 I spent several weeks in hospital with severe eczema. As painful as my eczema was, I remember enjoying being cared for.

My elementary school years, including extracurricular activities, were characterized by me trying to figure things out; always asking questions and constantly wondering about how to 'fit in' as part of the group. I remember thinking I was smart, and I knew I worked hard, but it never seemed to pay off in the recognition I sought from teachers and other persons in authority – and I had no idea what to do about it.

High School was filled with the usual stuff – football games, flunking Latin, boys and Army Cadets, student council, babysitting, summer jobs and helping out at home. I seemed to be always watching others to figure out what to do. The drive to belong, to fit in, remained as ever-present as an unsatisfied hunger. It was in high school that I remember asking my parents a question that would haunt me for the better part of 35 years! I asked them to explain the 'why' of something: what the rules were, who made the rules, how it all worked. I clearly remember my Dad's frustration as he said, "Patricia, I don't know. That's just the way it is. That's the way it always has been and always will be!" Realizing I was not going to get any different answer, I took a breath and had a little conversation in my head saying, "I don't think so, Dad. There has to be another explanation, another way."

All through my teens, twenties, thirties and into my forties, I searched for an answer to why things were the way they were, who decided the way things were and why. Things like: how come doctor's kids become doctors, lawyer's kids become lawyers, and so on? The inner sense of unease; the questioning and searching while I moved through my life and sometimes railed against 'how it was', never went away. But again, I'm getting ahead of myself.

By the time I graduated from high school at 16, I was already registered as a student at St. Joseph's School of Nursing in Cornwall, Ontario. I had saved the tuition fees from babysitting and summer jobs as a lifeguard and swimming instructor. Seventeen by September, a high school graduate on my way to nursing school to be a healer with no idea of who I really was. I certainly had no sense of me as an independent person or any idea of an overall life plan. I just knew that taking care of people was my vocation, verified by my Mom who said I'd been taking care of dolls and pets since I could walk.

I moved out of my family home, taking most of what I owned, and into the nurses' residence. A new start! I embraced my nursing studies with great delight and discovered something: my efforts produced outstanding marks and recognition! This was my first experience in doing what I loved, with passion and commitment. I was good at it and my patients often told me so.

In my late twenties, I began to notice that I would frequently experience waves of heat moving through my body, often at the most inopportune times. I couldn't really figure it out. As a nurse I knew 'hot flashes' were associated with menopause and I sure wasn't menopausal at 28 or 29 - and they have never gone away.

At the time, I was employed part-time as a registered nurse while caring for my university-professor husband and three young children. I was busy doing what I had always known I would do: be married and have a family. Not that I was taught in any formal way that marriage and children were to be my future, I realize now that I was never consciously aware of other options. As a high school student, I don't remember much discussion about careers. I only ever remember my guidance counsellor talking to the girls in the class about being a nurse, secretary or teacher.

I must have had other dreams at one time! Months ago, I was cleaning out some old boxes and found a newspaper clipping of me during a career day at my school. In it, I was introducing an Air Canada representative on a recruiting drive and suddenly remembered I did have a different dream - one of flying as an Air Canada hostess. In those days, you had to be a registered nurse to fly and flying was my dream for adventure, excitement and seeing the world. Nothing to do with bottles, babies and diapers!

Marriage followed nursing and while I worked, my husband finished university. Our life settled into a routine of family, children, work… and questions, always questions, and never answers that made sense to me. Whatever was going on inside me was ignored. I was trained in and lived in the allopathic medical model. So, the information my body was giving me, when presented to my doctor, was turned into a diagnosis and, of course, medication was prescribed. When I asked questions, the usual answer was - you've got it! - "That's just the way it is, Pat. Here, take this pill. That will fix it." Of course, one of the pills I was prescribed was 'the happy pill' and I was told to take one every time I needed it. Needing it meant anytime I was upset with what was happening in my body, including shortness of breath, constipation, abdominal pain, overwhelm, unhappiness with the condition of my marriage and with life in general.

For many years I experienced my environment as full of tension; an environment where I was sure of very little, where I was always trying to figure out what was expected of me so I could deliver 'it' I was searching for my place and some sense of where I belonged. I questioned whether I was doing "it" right; was I making a difference, was I being a good parent, a good wife, was I making the grade? For most of that time, I embraced the idea that something outside of me was always responsible for everything that happened to me. I didn't have any other information and of course, I expected something magical would happen and all would be well. My effort and hard work would pay off, sort of like the fairy tales we read as children.

In the absence of the answer to my question, I made up my own answers and lived many years of my life playing the 'if only' game. If only 'things' would get better. If only I understood my place in my family. If only my marriage would improve. If only I were smarter, thinner, prettier. If only I were a better parent. If only I felt better, had more energy, could get all the housework done. If only I could breathe more easily. If all my aches and pain would disappear, life would be wonderful, smooth and easy, and I would age gracefully and well.

When nothing seemed to go right and especially when my health didn't improve, I was frustrated, upset and discouraged. The future did not look very bright and I was not sure I wanted to be around to live it, especially if it was going to be just more of the same. One day rolled into another, with every day seeming like more of the same and none of it was much fun. The list of physical 'symptoms' grew and they were either ignored or medicated. It was a small life, full of rules and 'shoulds.' My body grew tighter and became more constricted and I was getting fewer and fewer answers from the medical system.

Sometimes life changes when you least expect it. One day a family friend mentioned a job opening with the local municipality. He thought I would be the right person for the job and why didn't I explore the opportunity? I applied and was hired into my first job outside of a hospital, the career taking care of people I had prepared myself for and expected to work at until I retired!

The job entailed coordinating community development programs for my hometown. I soon realized I had the passion and commitment for the job and also huge knowledge and skill gaps. When the opportunity for more education was offered, I chose - in a heartbeat - to go back to school, beginning my university career. What a year! University classes, books, homework, writing papers and exams - and me in the heart of it! The new information from the professors seemed to challenge and rattle everything I believed; everything I had been taught my whole life and everything I thought made sense of the world. The cafeteria became the gathering place: lots of coffee consumed, lots of questions generated and ideas debated. I loved every minute of it and my world began to change.

Over the next three years, I attended university, worked full time and carried (as did most women of that time) the majority of the load for homemaking and childcare. As my new career blossomed and I began to challenge the parameters of my established world, my marriage deteriorated. As I stepped out of the pattern of our relationship, the tension escalated. My husband, unhappy about the changes, struggled to exert more control over my activities as I worked to maintain my new found freedom and redefine the parameters of our marriage.

Many people did not know much about domestic violence in the seventies and I was no exception. While the tension in my relationship rose, I played superwoman and worked harder and harder trying to do it all and make it 'right' through sheer effort and will power. Somehow it was never enough! I was told "if only you would go back to the way you were, all the problems in our relationship would be resolved." After 8 years of gradually increased tension, unhappiness and violence, I left my marriage. The first night I spent on my own, a friend who had helped me make the final break stayed with me. We sat on a box spring (my couch) and talked all night. We talked about new beginnings; freedom, personal space, co-operation; peace and my passion and commitment to caring for my children in a loving, supportive environment.

I wish I could say that as the sun came up that morning, the freedom and hope I felt wash over me continued. It didn't. The uncoupling process, custody battles, court hearings and always being driven by my determination to be there for my children overshadowed the next three years, even when the children were split between their dad and I. I now had few of the lifestyle trappings my children had been born into and had learned to expect. I was consumed by my desire to keep them out of the middle of the legal proceedings, a process I knew nothing about.

I relied on lawyers to know and protect my best interests although they never asked me what I wanted. I wanted a fair split of our assets and liabilities. Three lawyers over five years never once mentioned my contribution to my husband's career; I nursed and provided for our family while he finished a BBA and MBA. He left our marriage with most of the assets and his pension intact.

While this was going on, I was juggling single parenthood, my job, university, finances and creating a new home for my children and me. In the late 70's, single parenthood was not that common and I worked in a male-dominated "old boys club" and was the only woman in the management group. I experienced covert and deliberate discrimination in promotion opportunities; financial discrimination; and experienced what we would now call sexual harassment. I was afraid to speak up as I needed the job and was heard to say more than once that I needed a wife. Most of the men didn't get it! They didn't comprehend the difference in our realities, the difference between having someone (their wives) to look after most of the details in their life, leaving them free to concentrate on the job. I had all the details *and* the job!

I did what I knew how to do, what I had always done: I worked, I went to school and I put my children at the center of my life. I ignored all the messages from my body, pushing them down with more black coffee or more work. Then suddenly one night, the fear, frustration, stress, overwork and the medication caught up with me and my body rebelled. The result was a severe asthma attack.

Unable to drive, a friend rushed me to the hospital where I received emergency treatment and admittance. So imagine this: I'm lying in a hospital bed hooked up to an intravenous, getting forced air/medication treatments, physiotherapy, breathing lessons - and I'm working on files that I had my secretary bring from the workplace! As I write this, I realize that at that time, I was so focused on ways of controlling my life - a life that was completely out of control - I couldn't even see the ridiculousness of my behavior! I was so determined to meet some unknown external standard that I wouldn't give myself permission to relax and get well, even while in the hospital.

Each time my physician reduced my medication, I panicked and had another asthma attack. I would have been there longer had it not been for my doctor who told me to reduce my own medication. Giving me control was a brilliant move on his part; I soon reduced the medication and was able to leave the hospital. With the custody hearing behind me and feeling devastated by the outcome, life returned to my new 'normal' of not having my three children together.

After several years on my own, having survived the court process and with the divorce behind me, I began to move out into the dating world again. Now I was 40 and out in that scary world of "what the hell is the standard now?" One day I met someone and life began to change again. I moved, secured a new job and began a life with a new partner. A partner who believed in me! I continued university and just before my 48th birthday, finished an undergraduate degree and was surprised and delighted to be accepted into a Master's program. Imagine me in a Master's program - wasn't that for smart people?

Even as life improved substantially, my constant inner dialogue of 'I didn't have enough, didn't do enough or wasn't enough', continued unabated. I worked full-time and worked at my Masters program full time. I was driven, telling myself that I was way behind. No time to waste! Get it done; move on to the next course, the next challenge; keep looking 'out there' for the magical elusive answer, the blessing, the nod that would finally say, "Alright, you're okay. You've made it, you're in the club."

I didn't think about whether or not I was really learning, nor did I take the time to celebrate any of my achievements. I was doing Coles Notes, the crib note form of schooling. I was retaining things well enough to pass the exams - as I probably always had - but I was starting to question whether I was learning well enough to own it, to use it in my own way or to put my own spin on it. In retrospect, I don't think so! It was all in my intellect and I was still using my intellect to silence the information my body was giving me.

My body and the genius within refused to be silenced and just upped the signal in an effort to get my attention. By now I had been diagnosed with Fibromyalgia in addition to my asthma, irritable bowel syndrome and, oh yes, let's not leave out my severe neck pain for which I wore a brace from time to time. The messages were getting stronger, in both diversity and intensity.

Not yet having found the information to answer my ever-present and elusive questions, I signed up for the next course in my Master's program and went to the first class. As always, I was eager to learn the skills, practice them and move to the next step. I was always moving, searching; looking for the answers 'out there.' Then another of those synchronistic events happened. In his introduction to the class, the professor explained he was also a faculty member of The William Glasser Institute. I had no idea what The Glasser Institute was until we got into the detail of our counselling theory class.

I was really intrigued by the information on Glasser's work and when the opportunities for completing an independent study by taking an intensive 4-day training program in Dr. Glasser's *Choice Theory®, a New Psychology of Personal Freedom* was offered, I jumped at the chance. At least part of my motivation was that the independent study was a short track to another credit and I was game for anything that moved me more quickly towards graduation! At this point, I was still holding graduation as the something magical outside me that would finally make everything right in my world. The tap on the head with the graduation cap would be IT - the magic to finally make everything perfect. What I didn't expect was that the Glasser training would provide me with the information to answer my 35-year-old question. I would get hooked and want more.

I certainly never expected the information would make such a difference in my life. The difference was, I learned I was the answer! I was the answer by being responsible for every thought I had, every word I spoke and everything I did. I learned I could control how I felt by what I thought and that the only person who could reject me was me.

Life got better. For the first time in my life, I consciously accepted responsibility for being present in the moment; paying attention to what was going on and living the vital components of the theory. I learned about perception and that my perceptions created my reality. I began to move from being 'at effect' in my life and living as a victim, to being 'at cause' and shaping my life. Einstein had said many years ago, "To be at cause is greater than effect." I was beginning to understand and I wasn't always happy about it. To be responsible for my life took effort. So much for fairy tales and magic wands.

This was the beginning of my awakening and although the magic didn't happen with the tap of a wand, it happened. It happened because I worked at integrating Choice Theory into every aspect of my life and life began to make a lot more sense. I carved out a path to move from an externally focused and pain-filled 'victim' view of the world to an internally focused or Choice Theory view. I began to consciously shape my world and slowly, my health began to improve. Finally, the questions I had started asking at ages 12 and 13 netted me different answers; something other than "that's just the way it is" or "just follow the rules and you'll be fine."

By the time I had finished my undergraduate degree, I was working part-time as a counsellor in our local Family Services Agency. When I graduated from my Master's program, I began a private practice. I continued my Choice Theory studies and a year later I was certified in Choice Theory and Reality Therapy.

I loved my private counselling practice. Having finally awakened to my power to shape my world, I taught it to all my clients, encouraging them to step up and take responsibility for creating the kind of world they wanted to inhabit. As I honed my skills in living Choice Theory, my physical symptoms all but disappeared. The irritable bowel, asthma, fibromyalgia…

they all went away; and if they did flare up, I seemed to be able to marshal my energy to manage the situation outside the medical system. I had long since stopped taking prescribed medication and now only occasionally used over-the-counter products. I did have back 'pain' flare up from time to time but life was much, much better health-wise.

A lifelong learner, I committed to ongoing professional development to ensure I was giving my clients the best and most up-to-date information. As I continued to take courses, I explored and chose to pursue a Doctoral Program in Counselling Psychology. Westbrook University supported studies in non-traditional fields such as psychoneuroimmunology. Studying again was a delight – more books!

Based on personal and clinical experience in my office, I wrote a qualitative doctoral thesis testing Dr. Glasser's Choice Theory with persons living with chronic pain. It never occurred to me to question the 'pain' paradigm; I just taught and then tested people's ability to live well with it, if they integrated Choice Theory into their behaviour at the unconscious competence level. I loved my work and when my results began to level off in some cases or were less than expected - less than what I knew I was capable of - I began to question and search again.

More synchronicity. While at a Glasser Institute Conference, I was introduced to Neuro Linguistic Programming (NLP). NLP developed by Richard Bandler and John Grinder was very compatible with Glasser's Choice Theory and training was easy to access. NLP provided the skills to help me to once again, create the results I had grown to expect of myself. I had taken yet another step in my awakening, discovering how to re-program a lifetime of ineffective habits.

As is my nature, I set about to learn as much as I could. This led me to the annual convention of The Canadian Association of NLP or CANLP. Intrigued by one of the presenters I met at the opening reception, I attended her workshop. The workshop was based on WEL-Systems® ideas, the work of

Louise LeBrun, and I was amazed at the results I had achieved in one short workshop. Another door opened – to date, the last and most significant portal to my ongoing awakening!

I was so intrigued by my experience in the workshop, I promised myself on-the-spot to find out more. The 'more' led to my choosing to pursue WEL-Systems experiences and certification as a WEL-Systems Catalyst® and CODE Model Coach™. My learning journey in WEL-Systems experiences has been truly transformational. Years of carrying around old trauma dissolved; health improved; self-worth was restored and belief in my unfolding potential solidified. I will never forget a conversation with Gwen McCauley, a co-founder of the WEL-Systems Institute. In conversation one night, I told Gwen I had "put my back out and was in excruciating pain." Gwen asked, "What are the possibilities for you, Pat, if you always think about pain the way you've always thought about pain?" I was stunned by the question and life changed in a heartbeat. No more back pain!

The one thing absolutely critical to my evolution - to my awakening - has been my steadfast and relentless commitment to my own curiosity; to leave no stone unturned in learning how to embrace the ache inside and replace it with the peace, joy and the deep trust of my constant unfolding. Curiosity about who we might become is at the heart of being human. Curiosity has been the driving force in my life. Curiosity led me to my awakening to the joy, passion and commitment to living life fully, every minute of every day, and to always be connected to those I love; my husband, children, grandchildren, siblings and their families and friends.

What message would I like to leave other women? It would be this: never give up on yourself. Never! Question, always question – and then question some more. If you think something doesn't make sense, trust yourself and ask. Keep asking and ask different people. Read. Go to workshops and learn. Learn about the quantum sciences. Be an explorer. Seek! Always seek the prize you want. Discover YOU are the magic in your life - and you will only find it within.

Patricia Donihee Ph.D. CCC - is a seeker and lifelong learner, committed to the constant unfolding of all it is possible for her to be. Pat consciously and joyfully continues to unfold as the invitation for her clients to step into their own unfolding potential. A classically trained Counsellor with over 35 years of experience as a nurse, social worker, mediator, workshop leader and trainer, Pat is a WEL-Systems® Catalyst and CODE Model Coach™; and Founder and Chief Operations Officer of Donihee Consulting. Pat is committed to leading her firm toward being a thought virus in the lives of all they touch.

One Woman's Life Choice

Céline Burlock

Vision Quest

I've always been fascinated by the native ways; how they perceive, see and relate to their inner world and surroundings. They hold every stage of human growth as meaningful and of great importance. They hold these human life experiences as sacred by creating ceremonial space to embrace the passage into new territory of the body, mind and spirit. The ceremonial event of 'Vision Quest' is one that comes to my mind as a metaphor for how I lived my life.

Vision Quest is a ritual-rite of passage that supported the initiation of a boy moving into adulthood. A young boy, between the ages of twelve and fourteen, who felt ready to proclaim his manhood would leave the tribe; go all by himself into nature and the wilderness; would fast for days, asking his spirit to reveal to him who he could possibly become and how by his unique presence he could and would contribute to his tribe. Once the boy discovered what he was seeking, he would return to his tribe, transformed into a man with an intention. Some would become medicine men, some shamans, others warriors and so on. The time they spent away from the collective of their tribe would vary but they would not return home unless and until they received the clear message from their spirit, mind and body of who they were to become and how they could engage that intention in the context of their own collective.

When I think of this ancient sacred ceremony, I find my life story greatly resembles a Vision Quest experience. My journey of self-discovery and re-claiming my power carries evident similarities to the ritual called Vision Quest. Although I was a girl, I left a place called home; had visions in my world of my perceptions of spirit, body and mind; felt the Fire of my inspirations including unfinished business and claimed it; and, when I returned home to my tribe of choice, I was a woman with a destiny and clear intention. I had the certainty that I could alter my stars - the legacy that had been passed down to me from my ancestors.

My Vision Quest brought me face-to-face with myself, to face my own Fire within. At first, I was really an expert at pointing my finger outwardly - living at the effect of what I held as the external world; living from the point of view of being externally referenced - blaming and giving power to all external people, events and situations as THE reason for my Fire.

For a long time, I carried the belief that God was in charge of everything and that I should not question that assumption. After all, I had lived through what I considered a challenging episode in my life. As I fell deeper into my 'victim-hood' experience, the less powerful I became. The less powerful I became, the more my Fire grew and as it became stronger and more noticeable, I felt more and more disconnected from the Higher Power that was presented to me. The Fire within me grew unclaimed for so long that eventually, it claimed my entire body and I experienced it as health challenges (which I now know was brilliant!); messages from deep within me sent by my body inviting me to start paying attention.

As intelligent as I can now see it to have been, it eventually became clear that it was up to me to be different and to do differently from my ancestors; to create a spiral of manifestation, not from my past history but from my present intention; to birth a new way of engaging my children and the children of my children and my own world, so that I could leave behind an era of new dimensions and perceptions of their world; to venture into discovering what was meaningful to me. How I would actually manifest all of the above was still a dilemma for me at the time. This chapter is written as a recollection of short segments of the unfolding into my becoming and describes how my world has shifted since my deep inner exploration within the crucible of WEL-Systems®.

In reading the following pages, you might notice images, memories, thoughts or waves of information as sensations, surfacing all by themselves within the depths of your body. These waves of information sometimes result in heat, tears or body movements like trembling or shaking. This is an invitation for you to breathe deeply, to relax into the experience and just allow yourself to be aware. This is my story - unique to me. Your sensations, being triggered by my words, will be your own story. This is an invitation for the beginning or continuation of your awakening on your journey of your own Vision Quest. My conscious awareness of mindfully choosing to manifest a meaningful future of my choice, to engage my life from a higher perspective, brought me to discover a world that I now see as being so brilliant and spacious. It is my intention to create a piece of writing that, when shared with you, may bring you to a place where you can discover your own life astuteness and the unlimited potential that you hold within… and more.

The Awakening of my Fire: Past Surfacing

When I first focused my thoughts on remembering and calling up episodes of my past, I can honestly say that I was not prepared. Nor did I have the slightest idea of what was going to unfold and most of all, who I would become. I didn't know what I didn't know.

The following pages will create a container for some of the content, or snippets, covering some of the events of my past. As I write this, I notice my body clenching at the thought of exploring these memories. I guess I still carry unprocessed signals - cellular memory lodged in my body. I know it will also be a wonderful invitation to initiate growth for myself.

The awakening period I recollect started when I had my first child. The beginning of my quest brought up new sensory information in my body that seemed so foreign and yet so old. I remember clearly the day I got the news that I was going to have a child developing in my body: I cried for at least three months. Feeling desperate/despondent and unfit for the task of motherhood, I felt so alone in my new adventure and too young to even be a mother. Somehow it was a question of trust; of trusting that I would be able to create something greater than what I had experienced in the presence, and then in the total absence, of my biological mother.

When for the first time I felt life in my belly moving and kicking, something unexpected shifted inside. I had become a crucible for life. The remaining months of my pregnancy held a blissful essence for me. When my son David was born, I felt this automatic nurturing coming from deep within me, propelling me to nourish, protect and nurture him. The intensity of messages moving rampant in my entire body were such that I didn't know who I was anymore. Nor did I remember those expressions of Fire in my body. For the first month or so, I was living my honeymoon with my new baby. My world was centered around him until that night when I started to have an extremely frightening and recurring nightmare, as if my body remembered something. On top of the remembering, it felt as if it was not in alignment with what I was doing in the moment. I had awakened to a world within that I didn't know I had dragged into my present life. I had a challenging childhood – and I had moved from one province to another, thinking and fully believing that my past would remain buried because that was what I wanted most in my life.

At an early age, I had made the decision I would one day leave; go far enough away to forget, thinking that I would remain untouched by my past. With the arrival of my son, little did I know that I was wrong. The door of my past reopened full measure and I didn't know how to deal with it. I didn't even know what my past was all about, let alone that what I had lived and endured was crazy-making stuff. And as crazy as this was, I know that without that past I would not have become the individual I have become today.

Now, with the birth of my first child, I discovered that who I had become was not at all in alignment with who I intended to be. I discovered that I was operating from my past, from habituated patterns that as useful as they could be, were those still deeply buried in every tissue of my body. Even when I was convinced that I couldn't intellectually recall an experience, trust me! I didn't have to – my body was doing a great job at that. Who I had become was based on my past and I was not happy with my present life. All I could envision was that I had to go back. I had to go back home; had to explore the deep structures of what was contained in my inner reality. I couldn't run anymore.

My Growing Up Years: Silencing My Fire

My growing-up years were what I would call demanding, for the most part. I didn't have the space created to allow me to be a child and demands were put on me to grow up very fast. I had to be an adult way before my time. Just like the boys from native cultures - around the age of ten. I was the first-born of my family of origin. My mother was quite young (17) when she birthed me and my father was 11 years older than she was. I cannot say that I remember seeing my parents being happy together.

One day, to my surprise, my mother just left. I will always remember the details of the date she moved on, leaving us behind to the unknown and what would soon be our hell. Like you don't forget when someone dies, that's how it really felt to me - the long hours wishing, hoping, waiting for her return, in vain. She never returned; she never actually took care of us from that day on. I was only ten years old and my sisters were eight and six. That day, I became the primary caretaker of my two younger siblings.

From one perspective, I was thrilled by the fact I was considered mature enough, grown-up enough to take on such an endeavor. At an early age, I learned to manage the family money, do the grocery shopping, cook meals, manage the household, buy clothes and all the school supplies for us. All of the things that a typical kid would do – right! I was also considered the hero for looking after my sisters, encouraged by members of my extended family to look at the situation with courage and hope. Often times, I would hear them say I would be so good when I married. I would thrive on the attention and encouragement I received from them. After all, I had enough shame on my back dealing with the ridicule and cruelty of kids at school teasing us because we were the first children from divorced parents. That was considered socially unacceptable in a small village of a population of around two thousand or so.

Soon I found out there was a huge price for me to pay – the one of being sexually and emotionally abused by my father; abuse that deprived me of all my childhood needs and most of all, my freedom of truth. I had to keep this big secret buried. My silence was demanded and positioned as a Christian action while our father became a practicing addict. He would be gone for days and I would look after my sisters and wait… wait… wait… for a miracle. I became my father's counselor, his confidante and his therapist, often stopping him from committing suicide. I also became his target on whom he could perform his darkest secrets. All of that, between the age of 10 and 12.

As the years passed, I became stronger - knowing damn well that I had to survive. No place for girly stuff! I exercised. I trained. I lifted weights, knowing that one day I would have to be the one to stop the sexual abuse. I didn't know who to talk to. One day, trusting my body, I opened my heart to one of my father's girlfriends - who turned out to be his next long-term relationship. She became really emotionally abusive to me and went on to physically abuse my two sisters. If I even thought of standing up for myself, she would threaten to tell our family my dark secret. I felt really betrayed. When I thought I could trust someone - because all I wanted was to not feel dirty anymore - it turned out to be my worst surprise. In my world, girls were abused and used.

I became as wild as a beast - uncontrollable and defiant. Because I started to assert myself and to voice what my body would guide me to do, I was asked to move into my uncle's house. I was considered to know too much, to be unmanageable; a threat to the two individuals who were supposed to be in charge. I was considered a 'family buster'. I was glad to move out. Finally! There would be someone who would take care of me so that I wouldn't have to do it. I was dreaming actually, because I soon found out that my aunt was experiencing a severe 'depression' and needed support to take care of her infant. So I became the cook, the cleaner, the sitter and caregiver, and the confidante of my aunt.

By that time however, I had developed resourceful strategies to manage these tasks very well, and I didn't have to be afraid of being molested. That was a relief for me but deep down, I was afraid for my sisters. Not long after, my father lost guardianship of my siblings and they moved to other relatives where they started to have somewhat of a normal childhood. That day, I resigned myself to live differently and to enjoy every moment of what I considered freedom.

You see, I grew up as an extreme biblical fanatic; a searcher. I learned at an early age that I had to have my nose in that book while I was growing up otherwise, I was told, I wouldn't find my way. Most of all, I wouldn't be the 'chosen one'. In my household, you were chosen. I learned that God was good but also that I couldn't predict his mood if I was acting not according to his law (which, by the way, was written on a huge wooden monument like an altar - the Ten Commandments - placed on the wall of the house for everyone to see). After all, we were the chosen ones.

Well, at that time, I had paid my dues. I was asked to leave home when I was not following the rules. I was raped by my so-called father. I was physically abused and betrayed in so many ways that at the time, my Fire was reflected as extreme hate against my GOD. I had done everything just like He asked of me, I thought. Yet, I had a life that was a mess. I didn't understand and I demanded an explanation. I went on to fight with what I believed was my GOD, having numerous discussions with him until one day, I fired him. I had decided that if any god would have created me and hated me enough to punish me or kill me, I thought - fill your boots!! I am done kissing your ass!

I believe that choice was the start of my discoveries of my culturally conditioned Self. I found I was living someone else's life – the life of my parents, my uncle and his religion; all of the people that I had encountered throughout my really young age that I had trusted and had allowed myself to be defined by their contact and their way of perceiving the world - as if it was the only truth and reality.

The only person in the whole world during my childhood that I would trust fully and felt safe around was my grandmother. It was she who became the presence that would help me to begin to re-define myself. She left this plane this past summer at the age of ninety four. She was my real mother. It was she who would show me that everything could be possible, no matter what. She always created an open, loving space for me to step into. Accepting, never judging, always smiling, with a sense of infinite compassion. It was through the crucible she created for me that I was able to make sense, in my body, of what being 'unlimited and courageous' meant. With the incredible amount of Fire I carried, in her presence miracles would happen, I would just be so calm. She was the inspiration for me to consider ways to become more for myself.

One Woman's Life Choice

At that time, that's what I needed. Listening to my grandmother saying I could be different, I would understand that I could be the one going very far in life. She always future paced me into expecting more for myself. I looked forward to more. I developed a drive that allowed me to tap into my brilliance at the time. I would engage in the most rigorous of tasks - like building houses! I trained lifting weights and I became so athletic and strong, feeling I was invincible. The four or five years I spent with my grandmother would become the years I will always remember as defining years for me. She made such a huge difference in my life - all because of her wisdom, clarity and her huge presence.

One day, my father remarried and I along with my siblings were to return to him. And we all now had to face and accept this new woman who was only about six years older than I. The dance of craziness restarted. This time, I didn't care to be part of it and I refused to be assaulted. At the age of 16 or 17, when I shared my dreams of getting a university level education with my father and that I would need financial support, he -sensing the distance between us and his inability to even have a clue about my world - told me I had to move out, go on with my own life, find work in a restaurant and do like everybody else, telling me that university would not give me anything. I just had to find a job. That was it. I was unwilling to be limited by his way of living and to have what he had. I moved out. I voted with my feet and started a new life on my own.

I was really busy, working at night and going to university during the day; paying for all my needs and being too exhausted to even play or go out with friends. As I think about it, I didn't have friends. I was too into my world of survival and didn't know how to relate well with my peers. I went on and got my B.Ed by the time I was 21. I didn't have any time to lose nor time to goof around. I wanted it all. I held the belief that life was so hard that I had to start living right then if I wanted to make a difference in my own life, doing it differently from what I had experienced growing up.

My longing brought me to find a partner at an early age and to marry him, move to a different province and to engage in my teaching career. Not long after that, my father passed away. I then learned I was pregnant and I didn't know anymore what I wanted, just that my father had left without ever acknowledging my reality of what I had had to live through. That triggered the journey of the surfacing of the immense Fire in me.

The Rising of my Sekhmet: A Call to Expansion

The genius of my body was carrying the exact experience of what I needed to survive and to live for my self. I knew how to fight for what I wanted. I knew how to fight to protect myself even if it meant I had to kill. Lots of times, I frightened people with the intensity of my rage and frightened myself as well. I knew very well how to rant, assert and how to project my Fire out. I was no longer abused and used, but I felt alone. Alone in my own world, not understanding for years what I was about. I carried the power to destroy – of that I was clear. People learned not to piss me off. I held the belief for a long time that I had to work hard and to fight.

Deep down, I was desperately crying; longing and searching for something more- another way of living. I could sense my fatigue, my refusal to live another day like that, yet I didn't know what else to do nor how to be otherwise. I just went flat on my back and was incapable of taking it any longer. That is when I made the choice that it was not worth it.

I left work, stayed at home, cried for about 6 months and began questioning. What was the point of my existence? What I now know is that the choice to stay home was what truly brought me back home. There was lots of pain and I could sense Fire everywhere in my body so intensely. I was burning! I was in rage! I was in despair and I was hoping for more; was asking, demanding and pushy about what I wanted to have. I requested some explanations as to WHY? I had done everything to my knowledge that was asked of me and more. I had put up with lots and yet, when I looked back, I was the one who had been shamed and turned away; who had to train to fight to even survive. Survive - not live. I wanted to be nurtured and a big part of me wanted to roar. I had lost trust in humanity all together.

The Still Point: The Day I Discovered my Breath

At that point, I became fully submerged in my venture of seeking, fully integrating a variety of practices seeking a spirit, body and mind connection; exploring, testing and most of all watching and paying attention to my results. I had searched for years and I finally discovered something that brought it all together.

I went on to take a program at the WEL-Systems® Institute and what I've gotten from it all has been so simple, and so profoundly life altering, that when I put it into practice, I actually could see and live the results I had been seeking for so long. The day I discovered that by simply paying attention to my breathing and changing it, I could actually alter my life was so much of a defining moment for me. I learned to breathe deeply; to anchor my attention deeply within my body; to follow the impulses, allowing what needs to move from my deep structure of reality; and to tell my truth. My wounds guided me to my life's task. My life has never been the same since.

When I discovered that my body was a magnificent quantum biological device and I actually experienced what that meant to me, right away I processed/metabolized huge amounts of unprocessed information in my body. I had a huge conviction that my own Fire was there for my own evolution, not as my enemy. As a result, I developed an acute sense of trust within myself. I could use my Fire to create a new life for my Self. I could process information in my body. I had it all!

All these years, I had been conditioned to seek outside of myself (god, authority, experts) for answers; for guidance to my next step in life, sincerely believing that I didn't know about my life - that Force that moves inside me. I believed instead, that I needed to trust the others to give me the key to my life. When the notion of living my life in an autopoietic (continually regenerating and self-realizing) way was presented to me, I could sense I was bridging spirit with matter. I could only see intelligence. For so long I had felt broken, dysfunctional; feeling the Fire of guilt, shame, fear and rage. Now, I could only see the intelligence behind it all and I was finally coming home.

Before that, it had all been about faults, broken pieces, wrong, and something to control and be controlled by. I had to control myself or I would be doomed to hell. I now know that trusting my body is where the magic occurs. The experience of that program has allowed me to explore and build a strong connection with myself. I've learned how my body was actually working. Believe me, it is not about what we learn in university biology nor in high school! It was way, way more than what I was told the body was.

We've heard about mind, body and spirit connection. I thought I had to work so hard because I held the presupposition that these three components of myself were going in separate directions and religion or ritual practice or philosophy would bring it all together. What I've discovered is that it was at my door step. All I had to do was de-cloak, open up and embrace my own magnificence.

What has unfolded since my experience with the WEL-Systems perspective -even today! - continues to amaze me.

My Re-Claiming: Dancing Life to my Own Drumming

> "This above all, to thine own self be true:
> And it must follow, as the night the day,
> thou canst not then be false to any man".

Hamlet, Act 1: Scene 5

Internally referenced; creating my life by my own design; dancing to my own music is how I now live my life. I am aware and so thankful for all of the experiences I went through. Without all of the experiences I have undergone, I wouldn't be who I am today. It became clear that I had a choice to continue engaging my life from my past (culturally conditioned, learned self and behaviors) or from the perspective of who I hold myself capable of becoming. I chose the last one and in doing so, I witnessed people who hold the dance of the past just vanish from my holodeck. There was no longer any resonance between them and me. I had altered the dance of the ancestors and the legacy was altered. It was up to me now, to gain a depth of clarity that would propel me into a future that was meaningful to me.

Re-Membering my Intention

I've grown stronger, wiser and most of all, more connected to my Higher Self than ever. I have gone on the journey to know My Self. I became clear and aware of my deep intention to hold the space in my world so that I can create from my Higher Self. I am unwilling to be a reflector of my past, of systems, of someone else's intention. In order for me to embrace daily newer information; holding the experience of a paradigm shift, re-creating my self; I have chosen to engage my life from a higher level of thinking; from who I hold myself capable of becoming. In making my choices, I know every choice I make has an impact on my unfolding. I mindfully, consciously choose from that point versus what I've known to be my culturally conditioned self – my past.

I now choose to engage with others to evoke their brilliance; to look behind the veil of drama and masks. Just like my grandmother was doing. I want to know people from the context of limitlessness. No need to hide or to protect. No need for things kept secret. What I've discovered is that I can create my own world instead of fighting or trying to change the existing one… or people. I choose to be true to myself, never betray myself, engage meaningfully and stay grounded so I don't lose myself in the external world. Creating with joy a lifetime of my own choosing, I am the artist of my own future, not that of my ancestors.

An Ongoing Beginning

Every day is a new chapter in my life. When I was invited to be part of this spiral of manifestation called Sekhmet Rising, I was thrilled and excited to share with the world who I had chosen to become. During the actual writing period, especially around old family stuff, I was aware that one part of me wanted to quit. Yet, another part of me knew that the places where I was still afraid to go were the actual places I should go, in order to claim my power. I admit this was the hardest task I went through: after all these years, realizing that I still carried residue of all these childhood memories. Yes, a few friends knew a bit of my story. I never completely covered it and buried it, yet "I" never shared it in the open, to the world. I am now willing to be seen; to be witnessed and to give others who have had a similar story some assurance that yes, everything is possible; and that healing is actually at your door, given a supportive perspective. Like a good friend of mine says: "We are not broken nor dysfunctional".

I am unwilling to play the dance of society with the labels of broken spirit, child or dysfunctional family. I claim that I Am Sacred, not private. So is everyone around me, if they so choose. No matter the story. It is up to the individual to change the dance. We always have choices. The choice of supporting the dance of the closed loop of secrecy is a choice in itself.

In conclusion, every day for me is a new beginning, looping into my intention of bridging what's above with below. My intention is to create a new era. I know that it starts with me to create for and with my three beautiful children; my spouse and all the people that I choose to engage with, a space that invites and allows for more… without losing myself. I am so unlimited and in that identity, I hold the possibilities in the palm of my hand and potential in the light of my vision. One of my favorite quotes that would summarize it all, taken from 'Ramtha: The White Book' is: "La plus grosse 'transgression' est d'accepter et de se soumettre a la 'limite'. If I allow myself to translate from my own point of understanding it would sound like this: "The biggest transgression is to accept and surrender yourself to limitation". The link in the chain of lineage to break apart from the loop of familial systems is the one that actually alters the craziness of repeated history. How much of your life have you lived from the repeated dynasty of the so-called family of origin? Does it still work for you?

Céline Burlock, B.Ed, is a seasoned Certified CODE Model Coach™, WEL-Systems® Catalyst and Reiki Master/Teacher. Founder of LIFE UNLIMITED... and Potential, Céline brings to her life's work a deep commitment and passion for supporting others in stepping into their unique and innate brilliance. As a catalyst for personal growth, Céline creates space through coaching and personal development programs that invite individuals to embrace change and experience accelerated evolution. Never turning down an opportunity for adventure, Céline enjoys raising her three children as well as spending time exploring the finest things that nature and life have to offer.

The Promise of Coming Home

Susan Bremner

Home was never a safe place. My father was an obsessive-compulsive type of man who always had his right place for everything. He had a way of standing over you and invading your space even if you were simply standing or sitting quietly. His overbearing presence was subtle compared to the ruthless rage that simmered beneath the surface of his seemingly kind and caring demeanor. His uncontrollable anger was expressed often in physical violence involving anything from hitting to punching to kicking to throwing things, with my three younger siblings and myself as his preferred objects of choice upon which to inflict these hurtful behaviors. And, if physical pain was not quite enough to satisfy my father's desire to release his rage, his frequent demeaning verbal assaults could always cut to the core of one's being.

I can never remember feeling loved by him. I felt only hurt and pain. Doing anything I could to protect myself and my siblings became my way of diligently operating in this unsafe world. My mother, who genuinely expressed her love for us, was weak in her ability to stand up to my father. Stuck in her role as the compliant wife, she was held in the chains of being financially supported by my father and deathly afraid of ever being abandoned by him. Although she always stood up to him fearlessly when it came to protecting herself from his physical assaults, she seldom took a courageous stance against him when it came to protecting us. As a result, I experienced helplessness and terror at the thought of being left alone with him whenever my mother was absent.

My father was an extremely critical man who expected things to be done exactly his way. I strove daily to be the perfect, well-behaved little girl who tried so hard to never make mistakes and to never do anything wrong. I made feeble attempts at trying not to entice my father's wrath. I adamantly believed that if he had nothing to criticize me for and nothing to get angry at me about, then, he would stop his yelling and his hitting and his humiliation. If only I could somehow measure up to his high approval standards then he would eventually grow to love me. But his aggressive behavior never stopped. And if I always tried to be so good and well behaved then why did he keep getting angry at me and hurting me?

After years of failing at being perfect, I realized that it must mean that deep down I was just a bad little girl. In fact, this was the essence of who I was. No matter how good I tried to be, I would never be good enough. Therefore, the ongoing hitting and verbal assaults by my father would never cease. I resigned myself to the role of always being the beaten up little girl. What if I could only hide who I really was so that the world would not know how bad and beaten up a child I really was?

School, which I absolutely loved, was always my refuge. Achieving a high average in school labeled me as a good student who obviously came from a good home. Yet, I was an extremely shy and emotionally sensitive child who sat very quietly in the classroom and seldom, if ever, participated verbally unless I was certain that I had the right answer. The parental rules that I carried with me into the classroom were clear. I was to keep my mouth shut and listen to the teacher. Ultimately, this meant that I was never to speak up to anyone in a role of authority. It was better to keep my head down and to remain quiet in order to operate safely in the world. In fact, I could easily become invisible, if I seldom spoke and if I did nothing to stand out or to bring attention to myself.

When I occasionally was courageous enough to participate, I would always experience dryness or constriction in my throat, racing negative thoughts about being ridiculed for saying or doing something wrong, and/or extreme heart palpitations and perspiration from the increasing fear and anxiety. Speaking up created so much uneasiness in my body that it often seemed hardly worth the effort. As a result, I concluded that it was unnecessary to speak up in the classroom. After all, I usually knew the right answers and I knew how intelligent I was by my grades. No one else in the classroom needed to know how much I knew. I could protect myself from potentially negative peer responses if I never expressed myself out loud. Therefore, not voicing any of my own opinions on issues became the norm.

It was easy and effortless to get by in this way. Similar to my high-level scholastic achievements, I always excelled at whatever work that I engaged in. Yet, being so talented and bright often cost me dearly in work environments with other coworkers who were threatened and unappreciative of my excelling so quickly. Over time, I learned to keep quiet about my exceptional performance. How often did I keep myself small and unnoticed in order to avoid negative recriminations from others?

No one outside of my home knew of the torment that had become a part of my daily existence at home. Not only would I never tell anyone, I would also make sure that none of my friends would have an opportunity to witness my father's behavior. I always preferred to visit with friends by going over to their home. And, if friends unexpectedly stopped by, I always elected to socialize with them outside of the house rather than inviting them to come inside. Being present in the home was dangerous and being outside of the home was safe. (Could this be why, as an adult, I would feel such uneasiness and nausea whenever others invited themselves over for a visit to my home?) Keeping myself busy with a multitude of extra curricular sports activities and other interests also enabled me to easily limit the amount of time that I spent at home. As the turbulence in my home life increased throughout my high school years, these recreational activities became a priority and my school marks gradually began to dwindle.

Although the painful bruising from my father's severe 'discipline' would eventually fade from my body, the verbal, emotional and psychological sores never had time to heal before being re-infected. My father always demanded that tasks were done his way and he was extremely critical and demeaning if they were not completed up to his desired standard. 'Stupidity' was not tolerated and was severely reprimanded. He had a way of making me feel annihilated and crushed. The overriding rule was to do as you were told.

What I thought and what I wanted did not matter. Speaking up against his authority and demands was never allowed. I would feel my throat constrict in pain and I would become motionless or frozen in fear. I could not say or do anything to express what I wanted nor express any disagreement with what was happening. I had no choice so I would shut down.

This stuck state of non-expression would unexpectedly surface for me over and over again in a variety of everyday situations and conversations, usually with men who behaved or spoke in a downgrading manner towards me. And the ability to say 'no' to choices that I really did not want was basically impossible for me. My father constantly reminded me that I would never amount to anything and that I would never become whatever it was that I decided to be. Therefore, he condemned me not only for what I did wrong but also for who I was. How could I possibly know the potential of who I could become when my connection to my own sense of self was being robbed from me?

I was accused of being the one to blame for his harmful and dangerous behavior. All of it was my fault. I truly believed that my being alive was to blame for the mistreatment that was happening to me and to my siblings. I felt like nothing; perhaps, even a piece of garbage. The unbearable anger and hurt that I felt inside me repeatedly rippled like a shock wave of emotional pain through my body. Yet, I had become very good at numbing my feelings and disassociating from my bodily reactions to his verbal assaults. I never wanted him to know the extent to which he was hurting me. Feeling nothing was so much better than feeling this intense pain. So, I disconnected from my body. This would become my usual way of coping whenever I experienced hurt feelings in my life. If had a disagreement with someone who acted like a parent and who was blaming me for something that I did not feel that I was responsible for, I would initially experience intense agitation and anxiety during the conversation followed soon afterwards by childlike sobbing once I was alone.

If I did not like the way it was at home - did not like following my father's rules - then there was the door and I could get out because, after all, he had never wanted me anyway. It was clear to me that he truly wished that I had never been born. As a young adolescent, I tried only once to leave. I was halfway down the street when I realized that I had nowhere else to go. I was alone, without money or a place to stay, and living on the streets did not seem any safer to me than being at home. So, I returned home with the realization that there really was no where else for me to go. I now knew for certain that I was hopelessly trapped in this volatile home environment.

As the eldest child, I always felt that the burden of responsibility rested on me for the care and protection of my younger siblings - a sister and two brothers. Taking care of them was important to me yet I could not always ensure their safety. My own desires were secondary to their welfare. This self-sacrificing concern and overdeveloped sense of responsibility for the wellbeing of others would become common place for me. Over time, I soon became increasingly numb to what I might want in any given situation and instead my focus was only on what others wanted and how I could serve those needs. I even convinced myself that helping others achieve success and fulfilling what they wanted was the path to having what was important to me. So many times in work situations, I would pass up opportunities for me to shine in order to allow others to excel.

During my teen years, my father's volatile behavior continually increased over the years especially if my siblings and I dared to rebel against his stern authority and maltreatment. He was determined to maintain his parental control and power. When numbing myself failed to hide the extreme pain and stress of my family situation, all I can recall is either curling up into a protective ball, holding my hands over my ears and screaming profusely, or feeling totally depressed and helpless and sobbing uncontrollably. Extreme anger and/or deep sadness permeated my daily life. Many times throughout my adolescence and well into my adulthood years, I contemplated the possibility of committing suicide. However, I could never bring myself to do so. What a coward I was. I did not even have the courage to kill myself. How utterly pathetic that I could not even do this right! Indeed, there was no escape.

Throughout my adult years, I fluctuated between feeling this overwhelming mixture of intense anger and rage that seemed to bubble up in response to even minor stressful situations, in addition to experiencing ongoing periods of devastating unhappiness and depression over life's misfortunes. Because I was trained in the social work field, I constantly used intellectualization and therapy analysis to understand and figure out all of the things that were not working in my life. I emotionally numbed myself whenever I experienced intense negative feelings that I did not want to deal with. I forced myself to feel nothing. Outside of my awareness, what had been wired into me as a child came back to haunt me over and over again throughout my adult life.

It probably should have been no surprise that I found myself involved with emotionally unavailable men. I gave all that I had - financially, emotionally and physically - to these men, thinking naively that they would eventually return my generosity and grow to love me someday. Yet, deep down, I knew that I did not deserve to be loved by anyone and, sure enough, I attracted into my life uncommitted men who leeched off of me and then left me. I soon resigned myself to the fact that I would never marry and I convinced myself that I would be happily single for the rest of my life.

What a surprise when I met my common-law husband! A caring and generous man, he genuinely seemed to love me dearly and wanted to commit to me even after a rocky start to our relationship. I relentlessly tested his love throughout our relationship since I was so convinced that this could not possibly be true. Yet, he continually demonstrated his love for me by daily displays of affection. It seemed safe to come home to him.

How I craved his love and affection and how unbelievably scared I was too. Screaming and yelling was my automatic reaction to any stressful triggers in the relationship. Panic attacks gripped me whenever he would walk out during an argument. I was terribly fearful that someday he would leave me and I made him promise profusely that he would stay with me. My fear of abandonment made me insanely possessive and extremely insecure. Sometimes my intense rage or fear was so overwhelming that I would lash out at him physically or I would try to provoke him to hit me and, when he refused, I would hit myself in the head telling myself how bad I was and how I was a nothing. When he stated that he could no longer put up with this behavior, I promised that I would be good and do whatever he wanted just so long as he would stay with me.

Yet I knew that my husband eventually would leave me if I kept aggravating him enough. I also realized that numbing my body, intellectualizing as a way of dealing with my stresses, compartmentalizing and dissociating from my feelings, diligently reading a number of self improvement books, and using social work self analysis were not effective in making things better in my life. I had exhausted all of my known coping strategies. What else could I do? Here I was, in my forties, with the realization that my life was no longer working. How could I get my life back?

Regaining my life began with reconnecting with my body. I learned to breathe deeply into my body with my attention focused at the base of my spine. I had spent a lifetime believing that my body was the enemy and that I should barricade myself from experiencing unwanted pain and suffering. Therefore, it was an act of courage and trust to invite and allow the intense energy that I was feeling to move through my body. I learned that this energy was stored information, wired into my body from years of programming from my infancy until adulthood. Once this information was processed or metabolized by my body, it would enable me to live my life differently.

At first, this seemed hard to fathom but I was at the point in my life where I knew that I had nothing to lose by jumping in and doing this. I was bound and determined to get my life back - no matter what it took and no matter how afraid I was! As I played with using the WEL-Systems® approach, I began to notice subtle shifts in how I was feeling and in how I was experiencing life. I suddenly realized that the life enhancing effects of this easy-to-use approach were just too good for me to ignore any longer. I committed myself to utilizing this as the context for living my life.

Throughout my childhood, I had operated as the criticized, battered little girl. As an adult, I continued to act in ways that displayed my tolerance of emotionally and/or physically abusive behavior. Although this had started out as an intelligent response to a hostile home situation from which there was no escape, it was an ineffective way for me to manage my life as an adult. As I engaged in Quantum TLC™, I experienced intense vibrations of energy throughout my body. I felt so much love and appreciation for creating this aspect of myself, amidst the tears of knowing that it was time to let it go. Then, finally, I felt a sense of peacefulness and calmness over my body.

As a result, I am now unwilling to allow others to mistreat me. No one has the right to bully me or hurt me in any way. I have gained a sense of personal power that enables me to walk confidently, with my head held high. I am also able to say NO to people and to things in my life that I do not want. Rather than feeling uneasy with the responses that I get, I am merely amused with how others handle my refusals. I finally feel that I am in charge of my life and that I am beginning to create the life that I want to have.

Intellectually, I was convinced that my perfectionism was the impetus behind my successes and my accomplishments. Yet, to my surprise, perfectionism felt like a heavy pressure on my chest that stifled my ability to breathe. Holding on to and living up to my demanding beliefs about achievement felt strenuous on my body. By processing this information, I learned that I want my life to progress with ease and effortlessness rather than with obstacles and struggle. I no longer put the same constraints on myself to be flawless in everything I do. I celebrate and rejoice more in my achievements.

I never realized how much intense Fire energy (that I described as the emotions of anger and rage) consumed my body. I experienced this as an overwhelming sick feeling in my stomach and as an intense burning sensation moving like a tidal wave up to my chest area. As a result of metabolizing some of this energy, I have noticed that the ongoing rage, the explosive anger and the panic attacks that used to permeate my daily life are now gone. Of course, there are still things that happen in my life that I find irritating or annoying, yet I do not feel the underlying explosive anger or the accompanying deep sadness that always simmered beneath the surface. Therefore, I no longer lash out physically to hurt anyone, including myself. I realize that I am important. I want to be alive. And, life is now worth living.

Like my mother, I had an intense fear of abandonment and given that I had never felt loved by my father, I also had an equally strong fear of being unloved and unlovable. I finally had to admit how much these fears gripped my life and limited me from living the life that I wanted. As I breathed into my body and moved into experiencing these fears rather than numbing my body, I sobbed in panic as I experienced the overwhelming movement of energy. I am now amazed that in those moments when these fears usually would arise unexpectedly, they are no longer there!

My strained and emotionally distant relationship with my father (although it has not developed into a totally trusting relationship on my part) has indeed begun to shift. I feel more personally powerful around him. The admonished child responses are no longer triggered in me. I can now stand up to him, as an adult woman, and verbally express my opinions to him in an empowered manner. And recently, my father initiated the warmest hug I have ever felt from him and with deep caring, he softly spoke the words "I really love you." Tears and deeply felt sobbing erupted from me as I realized that, for the first time ever in my life, I actually experienced his behavior as genuine heart-felt love for me.

It is interesting to me that a sense of safety and security was always an important consideration in both my personal and in my professional life. My home environment seldom provided the safety that was needed for the expression of my vast potential. 'Home' has now become that Fiery, safe place within me that allows for the expression of who I am and for the potential of the self that I want to become, to shine through. There are moments when I am still unsure if I can step out, express myself and be seen; or moments when I am uncertain if I can allow my talents and accomplishments and the immensity of who I am to radiate out for all to notice. Yet, I am also confident that there is an abundance of space for my own unlimited potential to expand and flourish. I have become a powerful presence in my own life!

As I stand in the presence of other women, I know to the core of my being that they too have the ability to reach their unlimited potential. In that moment, I realize that by awakening to their own sense of personal power, these women will have the inner courage to handle challenging life situations with grace, poise and confidence. Knowing that I can have an impact on inviting this to happen and being a witness to this unfolding in other women moves me to tears. My life is truly meaningful.

Susan Bremner – WEL-Systems® Catalyst and CODE Model Coach™ - is a National StarSkate coach with more than 25 years of competitive coaching experience. Under her caring presence and laser-focused intention, numerous young athletes have known the joy of discovering their own potential and attaining their Gold Test levels in figure skating. Skilled in performance enhancement and program development, Susan's background also includes public speaking and training seminars.

Susan holds a Bachelor of Social Work degree from the University of Windsor. She has 10 years of counseling experience, working primarily with the disabled as well as parents and children. She currently resides in Oakville, Ontario.

It's Never Too Late to Redesign Your Life

Lorna LeBrun

When my daughter, Louise, invited me to be part of this collaborative book project and write a chapter, I was flattered and excited. However, doubt kept creeping in, as I was not confident that I was capable of making my life experiences interesting enough to share with others. At 81 years of age, the experiences one has are sometimes not interesting enough to share with closest friends, let alone strangers.

But I say, "Courage, Lorna!" – and soldier on.

Approximately one year ago, I began preparing myself for what I considered to be a giant move. Although I had moved several times in my younger years, this would be different. I was downsizing from a self-contained home of seven rooms to a three- room suite nestled into a larger home shared with my daughter and family. And so, the cleaning out had begun.

Trying to keep only the things that I would need and that I would truly cherish, was difficult. One day, while cleaning out old letters belonging to my husband, Buddy, (letters to him and from him while he was in England and in France during WWII), I decided that I should read the odd one before throwing them away. The thoughts we had shared played an important role in our lives during those sometimes happy, sometimes sad and lonely years. And so, I sat in my sunroom with a shoe box full of neatly bundled, elastic-bound letters.

Buddy had taken care of these letters for two or more years while overseas, moving from one base to another. When the war was over, they were the first things put into his duffle bag for the long sea voyage home. It's clear to me that they were more than important to him - they were precious.

As I sat and read these letters, the words wrapped themselves around me and seemed to envelope my thoughts, my spirit and my soul. I became completely engrossed in the experience, to the point where many of the moments revisited became real again; hearing the sounds, feeling the sensations... as if they were unfolding in this moment. Needless to say, all thoughts of destroying the letters vanished. They had now become that precious to me, too.

As I relived pockets of my life through reading these letters, I became aware of how much my life has changed. Over the last 10 years, I've become part of a larger community of people who are seeking out more powerful and effective ways to create their lives. As a result, through time spent in conversation and experiences with Louise and so many others in a WEL-Systems community, my perspective has shifted. In the story of my life with Buddy – 60 years in all - I somehow have discovered that I was never solely responsible for the parts of our lives together that were most difficult to get through. There were two of us there, and neither of us came equipped for the task.

The Early Years

I grew up being very close to my mother, as she was to me. She was my greatest friend and most loving teacher. We could discuss anything and often did for hours at a time. I always felt cherished; felt that she was interested in ME - in what I wore, where I went, what I did, who was with me... a protecting and loving interest that helped form a bond between us that took years to get used to being without after she died. Maybe in some way, our closeness helped her to have something that she never had with her own mother or sisters and, most likely, with my father.

My Dad worked nights and slept days. He was never there in the mornings when I went off to school or awake and up when I came home. I remember that on special occasions he stayed up in the daytime and slept in the early evenings. During those times, he and I would go to band concerts, parades, exhibitions and all the other fun stuff that was going on in the community. He was always happy to take me places.

My Dad was a 'Home Boy' and had no family childhood of his own. He was born in England and was put in an orphanage at age 10. He and many others in his age group were sent to Canada by the boatload. They docked in Quebec City and great numbers of them were sent to a 'home' in the Eastern Townships where they were placed on farms with people in need of help in caring for animals and other farm chores. Some boys were well-treated; some were abused. Many documentaries have been televised on the subject.

As I grew up, I knew many of these people as they were the parents of some of my friends and neighbors. Needless to say, it was difficult to learn parenting skills from someone whose parents had abandoned him at such a young age. My father grew up without a father and had no experience of, nor model for, how to be a father to his own child. Nor had he ever witnessed what it is to be in a loving relationship with a mate or partner. You might say that they all 'winged it' – as parents and life partners. I learned to do the same.

I bonded with both of them on the powers of kindness, consideration and a peck on the cheek at our most demonstrative. Never a hug but always being loved from afar. Intimacy lacking. But you know, that seems to be the truth of what I and my friends grew up with in those years. I do feel that I was one of the lucky ones and nonetheless, I wanted more intimacy in my life.

I learned the power of a good hug in 12-Step Programs and have been practicing them ever since, every chance I get! In my WEL-Systems experiences, hugs flow easily and without discomfort or uncertainty. All in my immediate family are great huggers and I consider myself blessed. I love that about us!

It's too bad that I could not have created that for Buddy. He was brought up by his mother and grandmother. His mother chose to separate from his father (at a time when such things were unheard of) shortly after he was born. One day, a friend took him up to an office on Main Street and introduced him to his father. For the first time in his life, he saw his father. He was six years old. They never found a relationship until his father was dying in hospital, and Buddy spent many long hours sitting by his bedside until it was over.

Intimacy in those years was not easy to attain. I guess it was a taboo – a sexual thing; a 'don't wear your heart on your sleeve thing'. If you lived in a house where there were always people around, how did you demonstrate tenderness toward a loved one? When you were alone, what happened? With my mother, it was different and, what I've come to appreciate, is that I don't believe that she knew how to create intimacy with her husband, either.

Growing up was my training ground for living my life in a way that was extremely externally referenced, i.e. what will people think? So I tried to control it all. After all, as an only child brought up by a Presbyterian mother, father, grandparents, aunts, cousins – and this was in a family compound where we all lived in separate quarters but in community, in two large houses – my path was clearly carved out for me. My job was to be the Best Little Girl in the world (BLG) and if that's what I was striving for, I would *have* to worry about what all these other people thought, wouldn't I! Together, they designed and controlled how I should think, what I should believe and how I should behave.

Given that I was taught that this is how the world should be, if I lived my life that way, I would then impose this style – or at least, try to - on my children and my husband. Knowing as I do today that I can't change anyone or anything but me, I now think of things differently.

Discovery Continues

At the time that I was writing my letters to Buddy, I was a student nurse living in a hospital residence dormitory with three or four other students assigned to each room. Lights out by 10:00 pm so there were times when the last chore of the day was to finish my letter to Buddy by flashlight. His letters to me also were written late at night, likely under far more uncomfortable circumstances, with planes overhead and shell fire all around.

Buddy's mail was censored and locations were undisclosed. The content of his letters was mostly about what we would do when he came home, when we would get married and have our own home. Love letters – hoping, sharing our dreams, planning for a great future together.

The more I read, the more time shifted and I drifted back to another time. It actually felt as though all the years in between had disappeared and I was right there – reliving the past and those years that we were apart. I sat there for two days…. reading, thinking, often weeping, wondering why all of the simple plans we made for marriage, love, family and happy times together, never did turn out in that story-book style.

Today, through things that I learned from Louise about my beliefs, values and attitudes, I recognize that the things taught to me at home, at school and at church; by parents, grandparents and extended family that, at the time, were considered to be basically good Presbyterian values for an only child with red hair and freckles who was being groomed for the coveted title of BLG; guidelines offered for problem solving and happy living, all of which were taught to me in those formative years and in good faith, now suddenly appeared to be more of a deterrent. I had come to make the distinction between values instilled and values chosen – and mine had changed.

As I read, memories of that intended story-book life flashed into my awareness. I was transported back to the completion of my three-year nurses' training, nearing the date for my graduation from the hospital. Our plan was to wed 10 days later. After graduation and before the wedding, my mother, at the young age of 48, suffered a major heart attack. She died 3 days later.

Everything changed. Our wedding was postponed for three months. New announcements were printed and sent out explaining the postponement of the wedding day. Wedding gifts and sympathy cards were arriving together at my front door.

I was to have been married in a long, white satin gown, accompanied by two bridesmaids in long gowns. The wedding was to have been in a small chapel, off one of the larger Catholic Churches with a reception and after-dinner party at a local hotel. The white satin gown was taken apart and became satin pajamas; the other gowns cancelled, along with the chapel and reception plans. I went away to New Brunswick with a classmate to study for my RN's and to get away from the confusion and grief. I came back three weeks later, wrote my exams and got married the next day at a small wedding in the church library. For a moment, I felt soothed by a lovely, intimate reception of my classmates, close friends and relatives.

Buddy and I were off on a trip through Boston and the New England States for two weeks and home to our new apartment to begin what would become 60 years of married life.

My father had done all the things that needed to be taken care of after the death of a loved one. I was on an emotional roller coaster, with a heavy heart and the joys of sharing my prospective new life with my Mother – deeply loved by me and by Buddy – now a ghost of an intention.

We did what was required to close out my Mom and Dad's apartment and furnishings. We also set about moving our newly purchased furnishings into our brand new four-room apartment. And, as I was an only child and the only family that my Dad had, naturally, there was a room for him, too. He moved into our new home four days after we came home from our wedding trip.

I have no recollection of what those times were like, but I don't remember bliss. I know that Buddy too, was deeply disappointed. But instead of turning to each other, we turned to familiar patterns: Buddy went to work and out with the guys and I turned to bridge games and doing things with my girlfriends. Oh yes, and lots of puking….because I came home from my wedding trip pregnant.

Buddy went back to work with Bell Canada and was promoted to construction foreman. In the midst of all this, our new lives as Mr. and Mrs. L.D. LeBrun had begun.

At 21 and 24 years of age, and according to the wonderful letters that I had just reread, this was not the plan for our love nest. However, Buddy and I were so grateful to be settled in to our lovely new apartment and to be together, that our resolve to be happy was our common goal. After all, we were more fortunate than most. In those days, many men never returned. Others came home and could not find work…people died…

Between graduating from high school and graduating from nursing, at least six close school friends were killed in the war and three died of tuberculosis. My mother and the mother of a close friend also died. These were not happy times.

New Beginnings

We stepped into our new lives with a shared excitement: I was pregnant with our first child. It was not an easy pregnancy as I was still in shock and mourning the death of my mother. Also, the loneliness of spending long days alone after three years of living in a girls' residence and working 12 hour-days was beginning to take its toll. The puking… the loneliness and the crying… I was not a happy pregnant camper.

My Dad worked long hours, as did my husband. He also was at work all day, missing the camaraderie of his service buddies. Consequently, he enlisted in the reserve Air Force Radar Unit which took him away three evenings a week and most weekends. This continued for 10 years.

My classmates, a number of whom were still working at the hospital, spent a lot of evenings at home with me during my pregnancy. When they weren't there, my mother-in-law was, as was my Dad. It was great – however, what was not so great was NOT spending more time with Buddy.

That was the idea when you got married – to spend time together. We were not spending enough time together. I knew that he wanted to spend more time with me, as I did with him, but we did not know how to accomplish that without hurting a lot of people. I would have to throw my father out; get rid of my mother-in-law and tell my nursing friends to move on with their lives.

My teachings as a child told me that consideration for others ranked high in the making of good relationships with others. I learned it well. As I was an only child - and particularly one with red hair! –heaven forbid I should be a brat. Remember, we were aiming for BLG in the world. As a consequence, I would put myself last and my family there along with me. To this day, it is still hard for me to think of putting myself first. But I've learned that to do otherwise often results in resentment and lost opportunity – and I am no longer willing to live that way.

After 10 years of living together and raising our two children in my home town of Sherbrooke, we were transferred to Quebec City. This was a wonderful experience for all of us and it really broadened all of our lives. The children spent their teen years and early years of college in a bilingual society and I think we all have fond memories of those times together. It was a great opportunity for us to meet new people, travel and reconnect with friends. We had 45 guests from family and friends in the first 6 months we were there. Clearly, everyone wanted to see Quebec City and the Winter Carnival was very popular! I remember it as an enriching time in my life, making new friends and learning that I could be happy outside of what was familiar to me.

We would eventually return to Sherbrooke, some 20 years later. When Buddy was 63 years old, he retired from Bell. Even then, it was evident to me those 20 years ago that Buddy had some form of dementia. He knew it, too. I remember how he would spend an evening with his buddies from years of working at the Bell and he'd say, "I sat with a bunch of guys that I've worked with for years – and I didn't know who they were." He'd then add, "Non, the time will come when I won't know my own name – and then what are you going to do with me?" Not long after, Louise urged us to move closer to her and my grandsons, which we did 13 years ago.

For the last four years, Buddy has been in the Perley Rideau Veterans Residence with dementia. (There's an article around this experience in our lives, which I intend to write at a later date.) However, in my new life with Buddy and me living apart, I should add that our relationship has taken on new meaning. He does not realize many things in his life, but when he sees me walk into a room he smiles and points in recognition. He tells me "you're pretty cute but you're old" because he thinks that he is 22.

There is great joy and relief in witnessing his sense of play and wellbeing. There is also sadness, in that this erases many years of his life: the war, his marriage, the birth of his children, years of work and people who cared about him in 41 years of service with Bell Canada; his grandchildren, and all the places that we have lived since our marriage in 1946. And yet, despite all this, what we have gained is unbelievable!

His care is extraordinary. He has kept the humour in his life and as a result his caregivers are playful in their interactions with him. I no longer have the responsibility of dealing with him during his more difficult periods (such as bathing, hair management, dentist, incontinence, etc.). I just love him!

I have a social life with him and the people involved in making it so. The staff, the recreation directors; games of all kinds and especially singing; crafts, pot luck suppers, movies, guests entertainment , meeting other patients and their relatives, talking with the staff… they all tell me that when they work there for a while, they become one big happy family. I can see it and having been a nurse, I understand what they mean.

For me, it's all made possible with the involvement and support of my grandsons. I am truly blessed to have two such fine young men as a daily part of my life. Nick drives and engages actively in the events and conversations that are structured for the residents. Somewhat less enthusiastic about being a game-playing participant, Matt is unwilling to not participate in his own way. He loves being with us and just wants to be part of it all. Both are willing participants in the lives of their grandparents. After all, we've been a regular part of their lives since birth, and a daily presence for the last 15 years. They know these years are precious, having recently lost their other grandpa.

Had I not learned to understand that I cannot change other people (I can only change myself), I would still be struggling with the 'war cry' that drove much of my life: "How can we get your father to do (fill in the blank)." Today, he's just Buddy – and he does his own thing!

Were I to do it over again, with my added knowledge around the creation of beliefs, values and attitudes, I would start by putting myself first in my own life and encourage Buddy to do the same. Together, he and I would take care of our needs and then we would tend to the needs of parents, children, friends, things, etc. Had we done this, maybe we would not have lost ourselves and each other for so long, if at all. And I know that it's not an easy thing to do – especially when you're vying for the coveted title of BLG!

I no longer feel that Buddy was responsible for my unhappiness. Better still, I now know I was not responsible for his. The unfortunate part was that my understanding came too late for me to talk with him about it because of the dementia. However, because he, in his illness, is in his mind only 22 years of age, he has no memories of unhappy times in his marriage. Because he is almost always in a good mood, I like to think that memories of that part of his life are happy ones. We have a 60th anniversary coming up in November and I hope we celebrate it together.

And the Beat Goes On…

I still have relationships with people I was born next door to. Good friends in reasonably good health, in their 80's. People, who still love to play cards, watch sports on TV and eat out. We talk about childhood days and refresh our memories about how things used to be. These friends are mostly women who have lost their mates for various reasons, mostly through death.

However, the thing that surprises me most is their average age, which is 80+. We must have done something right. We are the smoking, drinking, partying, post-war generation. Although most of that group cleaned up their act 20 years or more ago, we still like to get together and play 'catch up' on everyone's news.

There are at least 10 nurses who make a very special effort to get together at an annual banquet, just to celebrate US! We, in my class of '46, are up for our 60th anniversary in Sept. 2006. The reservations are made. However, as much as I love that part of my life, I also like to move on. That I do with WEL-Systems.

I love being with the people who are drawn to what is being taught. I get to go to beautiful places, like Oceanstone in Nova Scotia, where we relax, watch the motion of the angry sea, watch Gwen paint her beautiful seascapes, see the gorgeous Northern Lights and eat the sumptuous creations that Paul, owner and chef of *Rhubarb*, puts together with great care and delight. It is indeed, a good life.

Of course, my reason for being there is to experience my daughter's thrilling presentation of Huna, the practices of the ancient Hawaiians. An ancient Hawaiian tribal ritual that causes little thrills to travel up and down your spine, and tempt you to take a peek by opening your eyes to watch this lady in her magnificence chant these age-old chants.

Participating in Louise's programs for the past 13 years, letting her new-to-me philosophy of a WEL-Systems perspective seep into how I choose to live my life, has made me different in some of my thinking from friends who have not had the benefit of this exposure to new ideas. There are times when I wish that they too, would read one of Louise's books, or listen to an audio program, so that we could talk about things and share ideas in a different way. I know that for me, my life is just so much better because of it. So, for those moments, I am grateful to all those usually-much-younger women and men who engage in WEL-Systems experiences and welcome me warmly into their lives. These others have been my friends all my life and will continue to be so until I draw my last breath.

I love being with younger people. I discovered this when I was 45. As I married at 21 and spent the next 24 years being a stay-at-home Mom, I decided that it was time to go back to nursing. I wrote to the superintendent of nursing requesting information on refresher courses. The hospital from which I had graduated had the budget to train three graduate nurses, 8 hours a day, five days a week for a four-month period, with pay of $89 / week. This was a windfall as I was trained at a time when we lived in residence, worked for room, board and our education, and we treated doctors like gods. Things had changed considerably but what hadn't changed was the camaraderie between nurses and the willingness to help each other and enjoy the art of working together to provide comfort to the patient.

Some of my closest friends, 60 years later, are the women I trained with and who are to me the sisters I never had. Hospitals today are no longer that homey, personal place but I put in 15 years, enjoying what I was doing; sometimes working with daughters of friends that I had trained with many years ago. They were especially kind and helpful to me while refreshing my memory and trying to cram in what was new after 24 years of being away. It was a wonderful thing that I did for myself!

It was during this time that I decided that I would learn to drive the car. I enrolled in a driving school, earned my drivers license and became more independent in being able to drive myself around. Last year, I passed my 80th year drivers test. I am very fortunate to have people in my life who are willing to do more than pay lip service to their belief in me.

I now share a lovely home with my daughter, son-in-law and grandchildren. My grandsons are ever-present in my life and we enjoy each other's company. I have learned piles from them! They have taught me that rules are just beliefs in action – and are usually somebody else's! They are WEL-Systems children - not controlled by shaming; not judgmental of others, not prejudiced towards others of a different belief; not externally referenced.

I am blessed with grandsons who are warm, loving, accepting and extremely humorous, irreverent and awake guys. Sometimes, I don't like what they do but I always love who they are – and they know that! I have never abandoned them or my love for them, and that love is returned in kind. They love their family and we love them. My mother taught me well: don't try to control your kids, just love them – and they'll love you back.

So, what's next for me? I start by looking forward to the next 10 years of my life. There are places to go, things to see and new people to discover! I know that in addition to life's surprises and unforeseen adventures, my life will continue to be filled with my family, my friends and the little things in my days that make me smile. I am always mindful of the important part that good health plays in living long and well.

In the spirit of embracing every day as it comes, I leave you with these thoughts. These are the things that, for me, add up to peaceful sleeps and full appreciation of a simple day. These are the things that support me in living my beliefs – I invite you to discover your own!

1) Don't eat too much chocolate!
   (But then…just how much is too much??)
2) Walk 20 minutes a day on the treadmill
3) Laugh a lot!
4) Shop a lot!
5) Talk to friends and loved ones often, on the phone
6) Give and gladly receive lots and lots of hugs!

Lorna LeBrun – mother and grandmother extraordinaire! - celebrated her 81st birthday in March of 2006. Increasingly more vibrant from one year to the next, her life is filled with humour and compassion; people she loves and who love her back; and a healthy dose of irreverence to make sure that she doesn't get too stuck in her world view! An RN by profession and forever in spirit, she continues to open her life to others, welcoming the opportunity to see and be seen along the journey of her life.

It's Never Too Late to Redesign Your Life

Reflections

If I'd Known Then What I Know Now

I would have relaxed and trusted the promptings of my inner voice as it reverberated through my body as the key to creating my life as an expression of the things that I am passionate about. I just needed to stop, breathe and reconnect to mySelf!

Anita Allen

I would not have waited so long before beginning the WEL-Systems® 'Portals Passages' experiences! The desired life that I longed for would not have been just a hopeful dream for the future - it could have been the life that I live right now!

Susan Bremner

If I had known that my Fire was my ally and not my enemy, I would have become the unfolding into matter of the full expression of my authentic Self much sooner. In all aspects of my life, I would have emerged, morphed, transformed and manifested from this higher consciousness and expanded awareness of Self. Yet, now is the right time.

Céline Burlock

Reflections

I would have engaged joyfully in all aspects of my life. I would have relished every curve of my feminine nature, every pore of my brown skin, every quirk and gift that I have. I would have stopped looking for the meaning of life outside of the ordinary, yet extraordinary human being that I am.

Dominique Dennery

I may have taken a different path and might not have ended up where I am, which would be the greater tragedy as where I am now is fabulous and is still unfolding as I go!

Patricia Donihee

I can only imagine who I would be today, given the strength that I now know I held within myself at such a young age. The possibilities are endless and HUGE! Just from what I have already experienced, I know how powerful my body is and that I can create whatever I want in life - and that belief is profound.

Karina Evangelista

I would have been seen and heard; I would have been an artist much earlier; I would have been awake to my potential and my value in the world; I might have made the same choices and I would have made them with intention. I'd be who I am now, but sooner.

Susan Griffin

Today, I endeavour to live my life authentically. Not just as who I "think" I was meant to be but rather as who I know that I am. If I'd known then, this would not be an endeavour but rather a naturally occurring event - and it would have been effortless.

Koreen Kimakowich

Reflections

I would have paid more attention to what was meaningful for me and included others from there. I would have said 'no' more often, hugged more freely and asked for what I wanted. I would have noticed that I matter, too.

Lorna LeBrun

I would have lived large, thought boldly and welcomed the opportunity to explain it all! I would have let myself notice all the things didn't work instead of looking away. I would have asked more and bigger questions – and let the chips fall where they may.

Louise LeBrun

I would have spent more time paying attention to what brings me joy and vitality as opposed to what others expect from me. It is in this state that I know I am fulfilling my purpose and having the most impact on the world.

Carole MacInnis

I could have unquestioning trust in my body wisdom, evident in my intuition and feelings … and I would have always been healthy.

Eva Marsh

I'd have discovered earlier that your opinion of me is none of my business. I now see that when only my opinion counts I am at my most playful, creative, productive, and nurturing. I sometimes wonder what fascinating people, interesting experiences and places I've missed because your opinion counted more than mine!

Gwen McCauley

I would have given myself the freedom to engage my life more fully with confidence and flare, and to ask for what I want. I would have paid more attention to my body and trusted implicitly my innate ability to create and to design my own meaningful life.

Noreen Mejias

I would have dreamed bigger, trusted more and believed with all my being that I deserved and could create an amazing, wonder-filled life.

Theresa McKeown

Instead of living in a state of fear and protection that led me to close myself off from the world, I imagine I would have been in constant growth and evolution; someone who was open to new ideas, willing to step into the unknown and discover new possibilities.

Harjit Shokar

I would have become more aware of my habituated responses and the effect it had on me expressing who I am. I believe everyone has something unique and precious to share with the world. If that is suppressed by what others believe you should do, that contribution will become small and insignificant.

Dorothy Spence

I would have done a lot more breathing; I would have looked inside of me rather than outside of me; I would have been more curious about my choices, and I would have noticed that my life is mine to create.

Jackie Zirpdji

And there is always more...

To find more information about the contributing authors, their websites, their programs/services and how to contact them directly, we invite you to look on the internet, starting with the page:

www.WEL-Systems.com/SekhmetRising

You will find information to enrich your Sekhmet Rising experience including free articles, an online newsletter, other books, audio products and programs to support your ongoing evolution.